UNDERSTANDING SECOND SIGHT

UNDERSTANDING SECOND SIGHT

Dilys Gater

CHIVERS
THORNDIKE

This Large Print book is published by BBC Audiobooks Ltd, Bath, England and by Thorndike Press®, Waterville, Maine, USA.

Published in 2004 in the U.K. by arrangement with Capall Bann Publishing.

Published in 2004 in the U.S. by arrangement with Capall Bann Publishing.

U.K. Hardcover ISBN 1–4056–3031–0 (Chivers Large Print)
U.S. Softcover   ISBN 0–7862–6765–8 (General)

The text of this Large Print edition is unabridged.
Other aspects of the book may vary from the original edition.

Set in 16 pt. New Times Roman.

Printed in Great Britain on acid-free paper.

British Library Cataloguing in Publication Data available

Library of Congress Control Number: 2004107019

133.B

DEDICATION

For Amamoa of the Starry Hair
It is more difficult to be than not to be.
Well done.

CONTENTS

AUTHOR'S NOTES

There is an important difference between the term 'Magick'—the art and practice of controlling the forces of the natural world as conducted by adepts—and its comparative poor relation 'magic', which usually means man-made or contrived illusion, even trickery.

This book is not concerned in any way with the practice of Magick and I have used the word 'magic' in a general sense throughout to signify amazing, apparently extraordinary or seemingly miraculous happenings.

Thank you to my partner Paul Gater for being responsible for magic every day. And to Simon Tansley for magical hours as my secretary and consultant.

INTRODUCTION

As a practising psychic, medium and healer I have found over the years that far more people possess spiritual and psychic awareness than is commonly believed, often to an extremely advanced degree. These are not always the ones who are taking an active interest in such matters, attending courses and seminars or expanding their daily lives to include meditation, relaxation, the power of crystals, colours, candles and all the various attributes of the so-called 'New Age'.

Most people come to awareness of their gifts on their own. They have no idea of where to turn for advice or guidance not only to progress further but simply to be able to confirm that their experiences are real and valid. They do not want to tell others about such experiences in case they are ridiculed or, even worse, considered to be suffering some form of mental imbalance.

It is for such people that this book is written. For those who know—because they have experienced something of it themselves— that there is far more to life than the physical. For those who want to learn more about their gifts and possibilities. And for those who are already aware of possessing such abilities but do not know what to do with them or how to put them to use. And also for those who may not have experienced psychic awareness yet but would like to find out more about it.

The spiritual and psychic path is a personal one, and for each soul it will be different. What is in this book is based on my own experience and the cases of the hundreds of people who have asked me: 'What do I do now?' I hope it will provide some answers.

Love and light

Dilys Gater

In Theory

CHAPTER 1

WHAT IS SECOND SIGHT?

Second sight is the popular layman's term for something deep and complex, the ability to see beyond the confines of what we think of as reality into realms and times that are not of this world or this existence. More than that, it is the ability to see the meaning and significance of all these in relation to our everyday lives, to have an appreciation of a greater spectrum of being than the humdrum.

We all possess this ability to some degree, it is not an acquired skill or secret information revealed to the chosen few. Nearly everyone has had some experience they could not explain rationally—a dream that came true, precognition of an imminent death (usually) or a birth, or even something as trivial as the sudden awareness that the phone was about to ring or what a person was going to say before they said it. The gift is intuitive and inherent, as natural as being able to see or hear with our physical senses.

Yet though we all possess the second sight,

not everyone wants to admit to it. Some prefer to find scientific or psychological explanations, others greet all mention of the 'Sight' and its associated psychic abilities like clairvoyance with scepticism, even anger or outrage. It is not the gift itself that bothers people but the awareness that they might not be able to control, or even challenge, what might be revealed. This is why instead of trying to accept and understand intuitive ability, many individuals over-react, ignoring its existence altogether or dismissing it simply as some form of crankiness.

The human race has always had a paradoxical relationship with the 'Sight'. Even though actively claiming not to believe in such things and that it is not possible to look into the future, human beings remain (as they have always been) obsessively fascinated by its unexplained vision. They do, however, also cling grimly to their right to refuse to acknowledge it if they do not like the look of what might be seen.

Mankind has practised divination and tried to look into the future ever since it realised there was such a thing as a future at all. This is itself is quite a sophisticated development for the concept of the future, future time, some personal or universal hereafter beyond the moment, something we take for granted, does not actually exist—or at least, it does not exist consistently.

So far as can be ascertained, animals have no awareness of future time and they are certainly unable to consider looking into the future as human beings try to do. Even human babies are born with no awareness of past or future as we commonly imagine them in physical terms. A baby does not experience anything except the sensations of the moment and even as it grows, cannot understand the concept of waiting until a future time: it requires its needs to be met immediately. A small child cannot actually envisage time at all, let alone as progressing forward, and cannot appreciate that 'tomorrow' or 'next week' will actually happen.

Until about the third to sixth year of its life, a human being is unable to comprehend the future and even then the child's perceptions of forthcoming events tend to be highly illogical. Imagine how powerful and all-knowing the pronouncements of adults must appear to children. Adults, they think, are able to look into this mysterious void called 'the future' and can predict weeks, even months ahead and tell the child what will happen—'Your birthday will come next week', 'Daddy will be home soon'. 'You will go to school next year.'

Amazingly, these things come about just as they were predicted and to a child this is nothing short of magical, though their own ability to 'see the future' in this way is something all adults take entirely for granted. 'The Sight' is actually only the power granted to spiritual or psychic 'adults' and yet to be achieved by less developed personalities, to 'see' further still. It may seem just as magical, inspiring respect and perhaps fear, but in the same way human children grow in awareness and understanding, the development of spiritual maturity will ultimately bestow on all the ability to 'see further' and be able to make sense of what is seen.

WHAT DOES IT DO?

Most uninformed people have their own ideas on the matter, identifying second sight with some sort of magic, probably black, with spells and witchcraft and other arcane and occult practices that are not related either to it or each other. In actual fact, what second sight does is—nothing at all. It is just there, as our physical sight is there. Possessing it simply means the seer is able to appreciate the wider boundaries and dimensions of existence and feel comfortable within them. Awareness of deeper significance and meaning make his or her life richer, more fulfilling.

Second sight is defined in most English dictionaries as 'the ability to see into the future' or 'clairvoyance', which means 'seeing clear' or 'seeing true'. A person with clairvoyant power generally has—to whatever degree—the ability to 'see true' into the future and the past as well as the present and to be able to read the hearts and minds of others, to know their thoughts and feelings. However the results are achieved, whether by ESP (Extra-Sensory Perception), by telepathy, intuition or simply luck, some sort of insight beyond the average does seem to be present. So can we sum up second sight as the dictionaries do, as simple clairvoyance?

The answer has to be no, because clairvoyance is only one of the 'extraordinary senses' that take us beyond the physical. All the sensory abilities we use on a material level have their counterparts in the psychic. 'Clairvoyance' (seeing true) manifests itself in images, symbols or mind pictures while 'clairaudience' (hearing true) involves the hearing of voices which may be in the mind or seem physically present even though other people do not hear them. Inspired or enlightened speech can take the form of 'speaking in tongues', sometimes in languages the speaker may not understand; other psychic senses account for the ability to smell perfumes or scents not apparent to others or generally to 'sense' the presence of the world of spirit.

But these are only the basic tools of psychic ability, the ABCs, as it were, of the real thing in all its complexity. Most people who possess second sight use it in their own personal and intuitive way, learning as they progress how best to handle their gift and work with it. Many formerly recognised methods of divination now seem primitive, barbaric or even plain ridiculous. How can we seriously relate today to the carrying out of existpicy (or hepatoscopy) for instance, in spite of the fact that this was very widely practised in ancient Samaria and was favoured by the Etruscans and Hittites?

Young rams were ritually killed and their internal organs removed for examination. This was taken so seriously that clay models of a sheep's liver, marked with detailed notes explaining the significance of blemishes and so on that might be found on different sections of the organ, were used as teaching aids—we know this because some of them have survived. And other gruesome divinatory techniques also involved sacrifice and the spilling of blood or the plucking forth of entrails, mainly of animals but sometimes of human beings.

All forms of divination are actually nothing more than rituals to enable the seer to focus his second sight more easily and sharply. This is not generally understood and has given rise to the popular belief that 'reading the cards' 'casting the runes' or whatever the method involves is an end in itself. In fact the method used is irrelevant to the possessor of the 'Sight' or even simple clairvoyance, since any of them will do. I have been able to conduct effective readings myself using whatever happened to be available, whether it was crystals, cards (playing cards and other kinds as well as tarot), runes, the I Ching, the person's hand, their handwriting, picture, name and so on. A fellow psychic paid me one of the compliments I have always been most proud of when she said rather glumly:

'It's all right for you—you could read an empty dinner plate!'

In fact second sight (and often the basic clairvoyance alone) make it possible to 'see' with no assistance at all. If the occasion calls for it or if it happens spontaneously I, along with many other psychics, work in this way. There are some practitioners who do it all the time but often the familiar laying out of cards or some other action that focuses the concentration can help.

MAGIC AND MYSTERY: Fiction or fact?

Second sight goes far beyond any or all of the extraordinary senses. It is not actually a 'seeing' at all but a 'knowing', a bestowing of awareness and truths that transcend the superficial truths on which we base the existence defined by our physical senses and human rationality and thought. In itself it does not bring about any change in circumstances, perform any kind of magic or cast a spell. It merely reveals information, but on the same sort of level as the most advanced spiritual wisdom which concerns itself entirely with 'being' rather than 'doing'.

Claims are sometimes made that it is morbid and negative to try and 'see' into other realms or divine the future because 'it seems to be all about death and doom'. But we know perfectly well that we will have to cope with problems, accidents, disasters and eventually death at some time and most people are ready to face calamities if they have to rather than try to run from them. So if it is not cowardice at the prospect of our life's possibly bumpy progress that bothers us when we look into the future, what do we find so disturbing?

Think about that small child who hears Mum say, 'You will have to go to the dentist and have your teeth filled soon' or 'Next year you will be grown up enough to go to the big school'. When her prophetic utterances actually come about—often traumatically so far as the child is concerned—then the child is in the realms of seemingly powerful magic. For in the early stages of development between two and seven years a child cannot differentiate between words and objects, thoughts and actions, what is said and what is done. In the child's mind talking about something is as potent as the actual thing itself. So when Mum speaks of a visit to the dentist, she is actually CREATING THAT VISIT, CAUSING IT TO HAPPEN.

As the child develops it learns to think logically and to understand the difference between thoughts and actions. But in the race memory of society as a whole these irrational childish fears linger, atavistic legacies from humankind's primitive past. Tradition forbids the mention of death, of disaster or anything we do not want to anticipate—not because we are afraid of the thing itself but because we are afraid that BY SPEAKING OF IT WE ARE CAUSING IT TO HAPPEN—or at the very least, causing it to happen sooner and more irrevocably than it might otherwise have done.

All magic is basically that which we cannot understand. Just as the child cannot understand how Mum knows he will need to go to the dentist unless she has somehow brought the visit about herself, the incredulous adult cannot understand how another person may know (second-sightedly or clairvoyantly) that a birth/death, change of job/meeting with a life partner, business opportunity or whatever else is going to occur. In fact the second-sighted person is using his or her insight and ability to arrive at a conclusion in much the same way Mum predicts that a visit to the dentist is imminent from her experience, awareness and personal knowledge about the structure, care and state of her child's teeth. If the child understood this there would be nothing magical about it.

Second sight, along with psychic ability and even belief in the spiritual, is increasingly dismissed by science as some sort of obsolete throwback to a past of superstition and mumbo -jumbo. There are apparently reputable authorities experimenting in fields like 'para-science' or 'psychic investigation' who claim they have cracked even the final, ultimate mysteries of life and death. According to them, human beings are now in possession of all the answers. Man has complete control, he is the final arbiter and so, ipso facto, no higher power exists.

It is triumphantly claimed that so-called 'Near-Death Experiences' are not visions of what awaits us beyond the veil when we die, simply the result of chemical changes in the brain caused by lack of oxygen. Even mystical awareness itself, including visions of God and all other kinds of spiritual and metaphysical transcendence, are, we are informed, really no more than the effects of a few blips on man's personal organic 'computer print-out'.

But whether second sight actually exists as what it appears to be or whether, along with other seemingly psychical phenomena, it will eventually be proved to be as organic as an attack of measles or pneumonia, the situation continues to be one of personal faith. All matters of a spiritual, psychic or supernatural nature remain unproved. For those who believe no proof will be necessary and for those who do not believe, no proof will convince.

Second sight—or some ability that passes for it—has been present since the beginning, recorded as having been practised, consulted and recognised in all cultures of the world. It has been referred to by many names in the course of history—sixth sense, prophetic vision, precognition or shadow sight. A disinterested observer would allow the sheer weight of evidence acknowledging its veracity to speak for itself.

Interestingly, primitive people have never had any problem about accepting the existence of the 'Sight'. It has only been when man started to 'think for himself', to develop the ability to question and make rational and logical deductions, to reject intangibles such as faith, that the trouble began. For rational thinking, logical deductions and all forms of brain-power are fundamentally incompatible with acceptance of the psychic or the spiritual.

If we start asking questions about whether it is actually possible to look into other realms or into the future (regardless of whether we think we might actually have done this inadvertently in a dream or in some other way ourselves), we are like a centipede trying to make a conscious plan about the order in which its legs should be used to enable it to walk. Any attempt to impose rational thinking onto an instinctive or mechanical function immediately brings everything to a halt. So we will only understand second sight and be able to use it if we accept it as what it appears to be and do not try to pull it to pieces to see how it works.

Various significant prophecies (examples of second sight) in the huge body of precognitive literature often dismissed as 'science fiction' or 'fantasy' are now quietly proving how very accurate they were, not only regarding specific scientific developments popularly foreseen by writers such as Jules Verne and H. G. Wells or by earlier visionaries like Aristotle and Leonardo da Vinci. What is becoming even more chillingly true is the prophetic vision that humankind would eventually outreach itself and attempt to set itself above any god or higher power.

MIGHT I HAVE SECOND SIGHT?

There have always been 'sensitives', highly gifted people who seemed able to employ their 'Sight' better than others. But the potential lies within everyone and if it is encouraged and nurtured it will surely grow in just the same way a child's awareness does. Sooner or later, if the child's development is not blocked or hampered, it will be able to 'see' in all the apparently amazing ways Mum can.

Anyone reading these words, whoever they are, possesses the potential to be able to see with the 'Sight'. But it is often not just—or not even—a question of being aware how to do it. The understanding of the gift and the ability to accept it in its entirety is what most commonly stand in the way. The philosopher Descartes said: 'I think, therefore I am.' But the psychic needs to turn this method of approach on its head. His standpoint must be: 'I have done it, it is done; therefore though I might not understand how it happened or even believe that it is possible, I have proved by doing it that it can be done and that I am able to do it.'

There is no such thing as anyone being 'just a bit' second-sighted or having 'just a bit' of psychic ability. Spiritual and psychic development follows a natural progression and will eventually be fully achieved by everyone as they evolve.

If you accept this as something natural and common to all, you realise that everyone, however diverse or even incompatible their abilities seem to be, is simply at some different point in their development. People who claim they have no psychic awareness are generally refusing, whether consciously or unconsciously, to accept their potential. They are usually, as we have seen, unwilling to acknowledge the existence or effectiveness of psychic power and second sight because they are afraid to face any prospect or future scenario they cannot create and control themselves.

HOW DOES DIVINATION WORK?
The simplest way for the ordinary individual to find answers has generally been by direct enquiry at the highest level possible—most usually by asking the gods. Early humans made sure the lines of communication with their gods/goddesses were kept constantly open and history is full of references to consultation with the divine, often on quite a mundane domestic

level as part of the everyday routine. But when extremely portentous issues were involved it was felt necessary to travel to some place dedicated especially to the gods—their personal temple or shrine—to present a formal enquiry through official channels. This would take the form of consulting the authorised representative of the god, his mouthpiece, the Oracle.

The priest or priestess who officiated at the shrine and acted as the oracular presence of the god was usually dedicated to the service of the god from a very early age—sometimes from birth—so whatever messages he or she passed on were regarded as coming direct from the mouth of the god himself. The representations put to Apollo at his shrine in Delphi were typical of this kind of divinatory activity. Kings and those of rank who could afford to do so employed their own priests, diviners and augurers who regularly acted for them when consultation with a higher power was necessary.

Apart from the gods, man has also sought answers from the spirits of the dead, usually his own family but sometimes more generally of clan or race ancestors. Those who have gone before, having passed through the hazards of life and death—presumably surviving them—become objects of immense

15

reverence to the living, not necessarily because they have faced their experiences with wisdom or strength of character but because they endured them at all. Anyone who survives any kind of traumatic happening, whether natural or man-made, will find they are popularly regarded as inspirational. Their opinion on all kinds of unrelated matters is eagerly sought. They will become, in effect, Oracles themselves, their words considered to be enlightened because of their close contact with death. So the deceased who have not only had a 'near encounter' but experienced death fully at first hand, can by this reckoning speak with complete authority on all matters of living and dying.

Animals too have generally been believed to have secret knowledge, as well as the objects of the natural world like trees and rocks, mountains or pools of water. Information is usually obtained from the dead via a medium and in the case of the natural world it is the shaman, the 'medicine man' or woman, who will if necessary undertake to venture into other planes and realms of being in order to discover relevant information. Seeking access to other planes and dimensions is hardly ever possible for the inexperience, enquirer. It requires specialised knowledge and skills as well as advanced spiritual discipline and these need not concern the beginner, though the role of shaman is briefly dealt with later in this book.

SYSTEMS OF DIVINATION

Does man have free will and create his own future himself or is the future predestined, already decided? The answer is that both are true to some extent and these seemingly contradictory versions of the future are reflected in the different types of divination that may be practised. We are concerned here with second sight, which is largely intuitive and which presents a general over-view of the future but is often able to predict specific events. The second-sighted person might say with confidence that: 'Such and such will happen'—and it does. In this way intuitive vision can reveal the ACTUAL FUTURE.

But a more formal body of divinatory methods concern themselves with possibilities arising from the interaction between different types of people, races or even worlds. The study of astronomy, numerology, or even palmistry, is not so much about what WILL happen but what is likely to happen when certain participating elements are present. These systems reveal the POTENTIAL future.

The assassination of Julius Caesar as presented in Shakespeare's play illustrates how the ACTUAL and the POTENTIAL

FUTURES find their balance and form what eventually reveals itself as both. A soothsayer who had 'seen' that Caesar would meet disaster on a certain day, famously warned him to 'beware the Ides of March'. In case the message was not clear, omens of frightful portent appeared throughout Rome indicating that Caesar was about to meet his doom. And when he arrived to attend a meeting at the Senate House on the morning of March 15, 44 BC (the Ides of March) he was stabbed to death by political opponents, meeting his fate exactly as had been preordained.

But what if he had listened to the soothsayer's warning—and the anxious pleading of his wife? If he had decided not to go to the Senate House on the Ides of March, might he have cheated fate and saved himself? This is where the full intricacy of free will/predestination can be clearly seen. Though obviously Caesar had a choice about whether or not to attend the Senate House, it might have been apparent to a diviner basing his predictions on the workings of astrology or numerology that his personality made it extremely unlikely he would ever listen to warnings or cautions from others. Thus, potentially he would have refused to see the realities of any dangerous situation even if warned he might be going to his death and instructed how to avoid it. So his fate was both predetermined and in accordance with his own free will.

The skilled diviner works by balancing all possible aspects of the future gained from whatever source and second sight can function completely independently of any formal system. But when the principles of such systems are carefully studied and the rules applied—even by those whose awareness is limited or who seem to have no second sight at all—they can produce uncannily accurate results.

CHAPTER 2

IS WHAT YOU SEE WHAT
YOU GET?

Whatever is seen with second sight will only ever be known to the sighted person unless they tell others about what their vision has revealed. Most people, especially when they are just beginning to use their 'Sight', want to share their information; they may even feel it is their duty, some kind of sacred trust, to communicate it to the rest of the world. And once the information, the vision or the message has been expressed either verbally or in writing we enter the realms of prophecy.

According to various English dictionaries a prophet is one who not only foretells the future and makes predictions or prophetic utterances but also acts as 'an inspired teacher or revealer of the Divine Will'. Few of us need concern ourselves with the possibility of being responsible for oracular revelations that will sway governments or change the course of history but it is important to remember that the 'Sight' is not something trivial. It is not a mere social skill we can pick up and put down, as it were, when we feel like it, or use purely for its entertainment value. The possessor of second sight is duty-bound to use it always as fully and responsibly as he or she is able.

Seers and psychics are sometimes assumed to possess immense wisdom far beyond the norm and may be consulted in life and death situations. One can only ever do one's best and speaking as someone with second sight I know we are all likely to have as many faults and failings as anyone else. But an awareness of the trust others may place in my abilities and the faith they may have in me, makes me personally very conscious that I owe it to the source that granted me the use of those abilities to make constant efforts to maintain the highest standards and live up to what I represent.

A DOUBLE LIFE?

It is the vastness of what the 'Sight' reveals that can frighten people and this begins to explain the paradox we find running through the whole concept of second sight. For why should the wonderful gift of enlightenment so often be regarded as an uncomfortable—even a dangerous—thing to possess?

The revelations can seem disturbing, even shocking if they come suddenly, with no warning, and if we are not used to the 'Sight' we have no idea of how to control what we see or are made aware of. And just one tiny glimpse of the whole—one flash of precognition, for instance—that is acknowledged and accepted as real means that as with an iceberg, nine-tenths concealed and out of sight, we have to also acknowledge and take on board the reality of the rest of the whole great mass.

People often try to quantify what they will or will not 'take' in an attempt to get used to the psychic slowly, as it were. To be able to accept the reality of something perceived as so far beyond our understanding, let alone live consciously with it, involves practice, training, a re-thinking of all we might previously have accepted as real, an entire re-learning of what reality really is. While existing in this other kind of reality, the one we commonly accept becomes itself blurred and unreal. It is impossible to exist in both—or more than one—at any time and it is partly for this reason that diviners and speakers of the Oracle were chosen from a young age, set apart, segregated from the rest of humanity. It is also why those aware of their gift of 'Sight' today will find they need to do the same to whatever extent and distance themselves from 'the real world' to explore those other realities if they wish to grow in spiritual maturity.

Two aspects of second sight always need to be considered. Firstly the vision, image or message itself, what is actually seen. Secondly, the way in which this is interpreted. The interpretation needs to be approached very carefully and this is where the skill and experience of the diviner comes in. There are many ancient tales of kings or other prominent people who, having experienced a dream or vision, sent for a prophet or interpreter to explain it to them. This was not because they did not consider themselves intelligent or canny enough to understand it but because they recognised they were not equipped to interpret it correctly.

Working with visions and occult phenomena has always been a skilled job for the expert, and this is why priests and priestesses were required to preside at shrines and why augurers and diviners were employed in civil life. The willingness to appreciate that being able to 'see' is just the first step is what marks the casual dabbler from the seriously aware. It was no accident that the ancient priests and priestesses, the augurers and diviners—and even those with extraordinary powers today—needed, and need, to submit to years of training and study to develop and practise their gifts: to devote their lives to this pursuit, in fact. If you possess second sight to any meaningful degree at all you will soon begin to realise it is not just an ability but provides the framework for a whole new way of 'seeing' and living your life.

We all have to start off as dabblers or beginners. We all have to be apprentices first, for there are no great masters born fully-fledged and ready to go, as it were. Either the physical disciplines or the spiritual awareness —or most commonly, both—have to be painfully acquired over a period of time. But in the speeded-up, quick-fix, instant-expert society of today it is often not appreciated how, in spiritual and psychic fields, a little knowledge can not only confuse but sometimes cause actual harm. It can prevent awareness of what second sight actually is and does, if only because there may not seem to be anything more to learn once the 'seeing' process has been mastered.

SPEAKING THE LANGUAGE

True adepts need to be aware of a sense of vocation. It is not enough simply to possess the vision, the gifts must be sharpened, honed, clarified, worked on, practised. Only with experience can they be used effectively and wisely. And when it comes to interpreting visions and messages revealed and given, the diviner needs to learn to be aware of the actual language in which prophecy is couched and become familiar with its subtleties of meaning.

The natural language of second sight, of visions and prophecies, is not the language we generally use to speak to each other. It is the language of transferred image, symbolism and surreal possibility. It is outside time and place as well as the human condition. For instance, when looking into the future for someone who is seriously ill one may see an apparent vision of troubles overcome and obstacles removed, of peace, prosperity, joy and happiness. The temptation is to assume they will make a complete recovery. But while this is certainly possible it is just as likely that the indications are they will die for in a cosmic sense their troubles would indeed be over and peace granted to them.

The diviner must not only learn to be aware of such possibilities but must be able to evaluate any number of 'true' interpretations and as with potential futures, use his or her judgement as to which particular truth is appropriate for that particular time and that particular person. A child cannot be told the whole truth about what his parents or other adults 'see' in store for him until he is ready to take it. They wait for the 'right moment' before informing him of the facts concerning, for example, sex, crime, adult responsibilities he will need to face later in his life. The diviner must do the same.

There is, however, one more paradox here for the careful interpretation of what is seen has to be balanced against the necessity to pass on images/messages/visions EXACTLY as they occur with no attempt to 'translate' them. Anyone who deals with divination and prediction soon learns that it is his duty only to make the prophecy, to pass on the message. He does not necessarily need to understand it—it is for the recipient to make what sense of it he will. Messages and prophecies must be given EXACTLY as they are.

All of this needs great skill and it is not surprising that confusions and upsets can occur. Inexperienced diviners try to 'read' the future to an uninformed public which cannot even begin to understand the subtleties of prophetic vision and knows far less than they do. Most errors of interpretation occur quite unintentionally with no desire to mislead—the inexperienced know no better. But if there is no awareness of any problem it is impossible for those who might need guidance in their psychic development to be challenged or corrected.

*   *   *

In spite of actively attempting to contact gods and spirits to seek answers, mankind seldom accepts the information he is given. He is often far happier if those who claim to possess the 'Sight' have to admit they cannot 'see' anything

—and he can become amazingly good-humoured if he thinks predictions have turned out to be wrong. Prophets are rarely appreciated and sometimes can meet with actual hostility even in this supposedly enlightened era. The more accurate they are the more unexpected can be the extremes of reaction they are likely to provoke, whether they are actively pursuing a conscious vocation or whether as sometimes happens, they 'accidentally' discover they possess flashes of random extraordinary vision and find themselves cast in a role they might neither have expected nor wanted.

New or aspiring prophets may well discover they are 'without honour' in their own familiar habitat—for one thing because those who know them will find it difficult to adjust to their sudden assuming of the prophetic or divinatory mantle. The public always expects the second-sighted to be different in some way, recognisably eccentric, certainly unlike themselves, and they may well regard beginning psychics as having suffered some kind of breakdown. It takes a courageous shift for relatives and friends to accept someone who has found a psychic or spiritual vocation in their new role.

The possession of second sight does not necessarily automatically bestow great spirituality or even sometimes ordinary niceness of character. Some of the prophets on record have been quite disagreeable people who were far more focussed on their own wants and needs than on communicating with the rest of the world. Spiritual development is an on-going process that never actually ends— it is impossible on this earth to achieve a state where one is able to exist as 'entirely spiritual'—and seers can sometimes appear amazingly petty and untouched by the import and enlightenment of information or messages they pass on.

The visions revealed by the 'Sight' allow us to glimpse the actual insight of the gods, their knowledge—like that of the Tree of Life— which mankind by his own folly has denied himself and which he has regretted ever since and sought to rediscover. But since the hugeness of the concepts revealed as the Divine Will/Divine Plan or whatever one chooses to call it go far beyond man's understanding, they may seem to threaten his very sense of identity and existence. Random revelations of the 'Sight' occurring in everyday life—of some traumatic event like a death, for instance—provide only glimpses, flashes, undisciplined fragments taken out of their context. They can seem like a door suddenly opening just a crack, revealing an overwhelming sense of some incomprehensible yet terrifyingly powerful whole.

The fact that second sight involves a 'knowing' rather than a 'seeing' means that the more highly developed the vision, the more final is the awareness of what is revealed. To 'see' fully with second sight means the vision of what is perceived is complete. There is no comment to make about it, nothing to say. It is a thing already finished with nothing to be added or altered. It has already been decided and everything about that decision is right. In the words of the ancient magi who knew the secrets of power: 'IT IS DONE'.

When visions of the future are genuinely 'seen' they are already (though they may not yet have happened) in existence—they already ARE. Second sight does nothing. It cannot alter what the visions reveal and therefore cannot be appealed to or argued with. It is absolutely final, and this is what can make the act of divination so awesome and to those who do not understand it, so frightening. The serious enquirer today—as well as pilgrims in the past who dared to visit shrines to consult the gods—is actually undertaking something far more momentous than we generally acknowledge. If we want answers we must also be prepared to take the full responsibility for all that might be implied by our awareness of them.

TYPES OF PROPHECY

Common criticisms of prophecies and predictions are that they are vague, generalised and conveniently angled so that they can cover all eventualities. Nothing seems to be clear-cut, assertively definite and any suggestion of shifting possibilities is seized on as a sure sign of inadequacy. But such criticisms only reveal that those voicing them know little about the nature of prophecy and prediction—or even the nature of the future, which itself is neither clear-cut nor definite and must necessarily be to some degree regarded as shifting and vague.

A seer is assumed to be able to look ahead at what is going to happen as though at a clear picture. He is assumed to be able to answer questions about the future with a 'yes' or 'no' and in some cases can do this, feeling able to say with certainty: 'Yes, so and so will happen' or 'No, it will not happen.' I am often able to make such factual predictions myself and in many cases, however unlikely my predictions might appear, they do actually come about. Practitioners can gain a reputation for being 'very accurate' (or not, as the case may be).

But not all predictions made will be fulfilled and many, with hindsight, might seem to have been quite wrong. This not only happens, but the seer knows that to some degree he can expect it to happen and it is one reason why most experienced psychics and diviners are not prepared to explain, justify or guarantee their methods of working. They undertake only to pass on whatever their vision reveals, whether this turns out to be correct or not. They will (if they are wise) decline to participate in any arguments or post-mortems if things do not turn out as expected. This is what, more than any inaccuracy or vagueness, annoys the general public for nothing is more infuriating than dignified aloofness and a polite refusal to be drawn. But public theory that psychics and seers avoid discussion because their supposed claims will not stand up to scrutiny is understandable since as we have seen, second sight cannot be equated with the sort of logic regarded as acceptable to the rational mind.

Anyone becoming aware of the 'Sight'—or any other kind of prophetic vision—soon realises that it operates by laws of its own, the first being that though the gift/ability/skill can be usefully employed for the benefit of those who wish to take advantage of it, it is not actually there to be of benefit or help at all. It has no need to 'live up to' supposed claims since it never makes any. It simply IS and each person can choose whether he accepts it or does not accept it. Whether people believe in, approve of or even understand the workings of the 'Sight' makes no difference at all.

'IT WILL BE'

The most basic type of prediction or prophecy can be expressed as a fact—'It will be.'

It may come as a premonition of some sort of happening or incident, whether traumatic or not; awareness or foreknowledge of anything likely to occur in the natural order of events. It may come in answer to a specific question or unprompted—'Yes, you will marry,' or 'You will have two children,' for example.

It may also concern an outcome—'Yes, your business deal will be successfully negotiated' or 'Yes, your house will be sold.

All questions dealing with facts—whether so and so will happen, whether it will come about in such and such a way—can be predicted simply and with no vagueness at all if the answer is actually 'seen', though sometimes no such answer can be given. There is no confusion or vagueness if a fact or a 'yes or no' is involved and in most cases these are the kind of predictions which do come about exactly as they have been foretold. Vagueness can arise when the prediction or vision has to be qualified, when 'It will be' becomes 'It may be'.

'IT MAY BE'

Some events will happen and there is nothing anyone can do to alter them. Natural disasters, certain traumatic experiences in each person's life—these are fated, they have to be accepted and overcome and cannot be avoided. But sometimes the diviner or prophet cannot be sure. And questions like: 'Will I be happy?' 'Will I be successful?' cannot always be answered in one word. We enter the realms of relative values where simple clairvoyance is often not enough.

'Yes, you will be successful,' says the seer, who perceives quite clearly that the enquirer will end up a millionaire at the age of thirty-five. But the vision may not always reveal subtler aspects—that his fortune will have been made from the exploitation of others and that though materially successful, he will be hated by all who come into contact with him.

If the enquirer was to choose instead to address his inherent selfishness and greed and so fail to acquire a fortune, would that mean he should be classed as a failure? He might end up more modestly with regard to finance, but be celebrated as one of his hometown's most respected and admired sons. It could still be correctly predicted that 'You will be successful in what you do.'

When the seer sees that such and such a thing MAY happen, we enter the realms of the potential where the development of the personality, spiritual growth and the personal and spiritual development of others has a part to play. The course of the future is affected by the attitude one adopts towards it: sometimes the scenario I have seen for a sitter has been quite a definite one but has been heavily dependent on whether the person concerned would overcome their own personal bogey. The characteristics inherent in someone's personality indicate whether they will be able to attain their potential future by making the effort or not, and the 'Sight' also reveals information about how far the personality has progressed, whether it is actually ready to move on to the future that awaits it or whether the time is not yet right. In some cases it is even possible to 'see', to a certain extent, how long it will be before the moment will come when the individual will be able to move forward.

Even if the person making enquiries about his or her future is only concerned with one particular aspect of it, the seer needs to be aware of such complexities and of problems that may be blocking emotional and spiritual progress should these reveal themselves. I often find I get a clear picture of a sitter's psychological state, how it came about, the alternative paths that lie ahead and which path the individual will probably take at any given moment. After much thought and deliberation I made a conscious decision to speak as openly to those who consulted me as seemed appropriate for them about their situation even though the attitude of a psychiatrist would be to let people work their way through themselves.

I have found without exception that when I have actually told the person concerned what I have seen, how things happened to cause their problems and what they can do about it, the results have been entirely positive and beneficial, often (though not always) producing a dramatic breakthrough. But one has to be extremely careful and never be judgmental. The enthusiastic novice is more likely to create more problems by trying to apply visions of the 'Sight' as a universal answer that must be just as enthusiastically accepted by everyone else. Always respect the personal vision of others, however limited it might seem to you.

'I CAN SEE BUT NOT UNDERSTAND OR TELL YOU'

All the visions and insights perceived with second sight are intuitively clear to the seer, not because they make sense but because they are also perceived as part of an inherent truth which IS and therefore needs no explanation even if the seer himself cannot understand it. Sometimes it may not seem to make any sense that can be recognised at all but it must still be given exactly as it is perceived and the seer learns not to try to interfere with the vision, however great the temptation to do so. It is only with hindsight that prophecies and predictions of this kind can be seen to have actually been accurate, and in what way.

With the gift of vision there generally comes the ability for the seer to accept the inevitability of what is perceived, however potentially upsetting. Prophets can pass on the most traumatic messages without being personally affected by them and this is why apocalyptic visions that might seriously frighten the average human being are likely to leave the seer untroubled.

Sometimes what is seen—and the type of prediction or prophecy that needs to be made—cannot be communicated to others by means of words at all. Words may be used but as a form of communication, they may actually only obscure the truth of what is said.

What is seen exists—sometimes only superficially but often to a very significant degree—on other levels to the one where we

37

conduct our normal communications and measure our reality. Some answers cannot be given, though they are there, except in the language of prophetic symbolism itself. And sometimes the visions or messages are so complex that though the seer intuitively grasps the whole meaning he cannot even begin to relate it to others.

The prophetic visions may be such that they cannot possibly be described or reported in finite language, even if they are concerned with future events for some particular person. They may contain immense possibilities, like a mathematical formula. And while many beginners are thrilled and excited if they are given a glimpse through the half-opened doorway of extraordinary awareness and want to share their experiences, trying to find words to describe what they have seen, seers and diviners who have progressed further along the spiritual path know that it becomes increasingly impossible to do so.

The language of the 'Sight', of prophecies and predictions, inevitably takes the adept beyond mere words and even, on the deepest (or highest) level, beyond images, possibilities and suggestions of the mind. The deepest (or highest) revelation—and the only way it can be communicated—is silence, but a silence that is not what we understand as simply the absence of sound. The greatest seers and prophets of all time have been notable not only for what they said but for their silences too and the fact that so many prophecies are in riddles, in paradoxes, in puzzling symbols only reflects this. Trying to pin down a wider context that the seer can hardly even begin to appreciate himself in the letters and shapes of words, inevitably ends by being trite, superficial, childishly emotive or otherwise limiting.

The only really accurate language there can be of prediction and prophecy, ultimately, is that of shared awareness between minds, where there is no need of explanation and where because everything is understood and accepted as truth itself, basic elements like mistaken meaning or errors of interpretation cannot occur.

FINDING THE WORDS

It would be almost impossible to invent prophecies, try to fake them on anything like a regular basis for inventiveness would soon flag and imagination exhaust itself. Most of what is claimed to be fakery in this kind of field is not intended but comes about as genuine vision distorted by garbled addition or interpretive comment, often overlaid by the seer's own personal opinion, bias or attitude to what he or she 'sees'.

The language in which predictions and prophecies are made needs a little further clarification. Biblical or other ritual language often seems to be used and messages purporting to come from a divine or highly spiritual source may seem extremely trite and trivial—accounts of messages received at seances, for instance, have become clichés in this connection. 'Channelled' texts and supposed spirit communications may also appear rather ridiculous in the language in which they are expressed.

Enlightened teaching and great wisdom can just as easily be conveyed in very simple terms as in some complex manner. But what can cause problems is that whatever the source, we may well find it difficult to take any messages or visions seriously when they are expressed in language we not only would not expect to be used but actually find laughable or silly. The reason why this happens is that most visions, images and messages are perceived intuitively. The seer or prophet, even the medium, not only has to act as a receiver but has to translate what they perceive into language that will make it comprehensible. Though this is done unconsciously, the limitations of that person's brain and vocabulary will influence the result. Since in the western world most people have been influenced by Christian teachings, Biblical phraseology is most likely to appear when spiritual matters are being discussed, or sometimes the sort of Victorian sentiment the individual concerned might personally regard as beautiful and elevated.

We have to remember that: 'The messenger is not the message.'

*   *   *

But if most of us are not aware of the advanced skills of prophetic interpretation what possible test can we apply to whatever might be presented to us to check whether it is genuine? There have always been dire warning about 'false prophets' and the nature of prophecy itself and the language in which it speaks leaves the whole field of seership and prediction vulnerable to possible fakery, whether deliberate or as a result of unintentional error. Is there any way we can differentiate between a genuine seer or prophet and someone who might be deluded, even 'seeing things' in a medical/clinical sense, hallucinating or otherwise expressing symptoms of mental/physical imbalance or illness? Even more important, how can we ourselves differentiate between what we might experience as second sight and phenomena brought on by our own physical state, imagination or wishful thinking? The beginner soon finds that the most common problem

41

when working with second sight is the tendency of one's rational brain to query and doubt the whole experience.

The word 'imbalance' holds the answer for the true test of second sight is that everything it reveals is so finely balanced that, while being completely unaffected by personal feeling or any sense of moral judgement, it nevertheless speaks to us in tones of complete and utter truth. We will always react to the genuine vision, if we face it honestly, by admitting: 'Yes, this is something I have always known.' For even though the future may not yet have happened it not only already exists but in the depths of our unconscious WE ALREADY KNOW WHAT IT IS.

We generally assume the way to evaluate a prophecy is to ask ourselves, first, what it means and, then, when we understand its content, wait to see whether it comes true or not. But since it is often not possible to express the meaning of a prophecy except in the symbolism of prophetic language itself and because the vision involves an awareness of something already complete and final there is really no question about whether it will 'come true'. The flowery language of the ancients expressed it best when they concerned themselves not with visions 'coming true' but with fulfilment at the appropriate time.

To the seer, past, present and future are equally significant and relevant. In this awareness then, it does not matter exactly when, it what order, at what time, events take place for in the language of prophecy everything that ever happens has, does and will occur 'in due time'—when the appropriate moment comes.

In Practice

CHAPTER 3

OPEN YOUR EYES

Before you begin consciously developing and working with your innate power of 'sight', you need to be aware that the boundaries you have previously accepted as real must be lifted. To 'see' is to be willing to look at anything and everything AS IT IS, not as you thought it was or as it ought to be, or even as you imagine it will be when you view it with 'other sight'.

You must also be prepared to proceed beyond the methods of communication with which you have previously been familiar. You will become aware of the most basic concepts of 'second sight' which are that:

TO SEE IS TO KNOW
TO KNOW IS TO UNDERSTAND
THAT THERE IS NO NEED TO TRY
  EITHER TO SEE OR KNOW

True 'seeing' is not an achievement, it is in fact a relinquishing of all effort, of trying to make things happen. Instead of a doing, it is a

45

relaxing, a letting things happen or not, as they will. And there is no need either to feel constrained to describe what you might see or know to others. You do not have any obligation to persuade them to accept and share your own realities.

EVERYTHING IS DIFFERENT—
EVERYTHING IS THE SAME

Nothing changes, yet everything changes. This is the paradox of seeing with the 'Sight'. And one of the things you will become aware of is that while the 'Sight' does not look at life in an 'ordinary' way, it is actually nothing but a reflection of what you have been aware of all along, just beyond the shapes of what is considered 'ordinary' and real. It is another way of describing the intangibles that have always made up the true reality: the concepts inherent in all art and science, mathematics, physics, music and literature.

The first step towards using your 'sight' is to begin spending time just opening your mind. You can do this in daily meditation on your own but more usefully you can make it informal, a part of your everyday living—try opening your mind while waiting in a bus queue or at the launderette for instance.

Take some comment on philosophy or the nature of reality like the ones quoted below and just let it drift through your mind, examining it without trying to make sense of it or apply it. Make no effort to agree or disagree, do not allow yourself to form opinions or make judgements. The kind of 'thought for the day' that can be found in a good diary or calendar is ideal or you can dip into collections of quotations or proverbs, poetry or any kind of 'sayings'.

*   *   *

'Man can embody truth, but he cannot know it'
W. B. Yeats

'Creative writers . . . are apt to know a whole host of things between heaven and earth of which our philosophy has not yet let us dream. In their knowledge of the mind they are far in advance of us everyday people for they draw upon sources which we have not yet opened up for science.'
Sigmund Freud: DELUSIONS AND
DREAMS IN JENSEN'S GRADIVA

'Any power that is wielded over you is non-existent.'
Yvaine Huath

'The clairvoyant reality leads as inexorably to personal, self-aware survival of biological death as the sensory reality leads to annihilation.'
Lawrence LeShan: ALTERNATE REALITIES: THE SEARCH FOR THE FULL HUMAN BEING

'Our birth is but a sleep and a forgetting: The Soul that rises with us, our life's Star, Hath had elsewhere its setting, And cometh from afar.'
William Wordsworth: ODE ON THE INTIMATIONS OF IMMORTALITY

'The symbol . . . arises as a consequence of distancing or detaching the self from the object . . . a symbol makes it possible for us to form conceptions of objects . . . The symbol, therefore, increases our grasp and mastery of reality.'
Anthony Storr: THE DYNAMICS OF CREATION

*   *   *

Once you have begun to allow your thoughts just to drift and are on your way to expanding your awareness, you will find that things begin to happen in your sense of reality without your making any effort. Just be prepared for whatever comes and do not make any attempt to control or organise what you perceive.

It is important that you do not allow (or even encourage) yourself to float off mentally and lose yourself in what you might envisage as some kind of superior, spiritual way of thinking. Or even try to be too aware. All realities are equal if we accept them. So whether your bus is coming or you need to put your laundry into the drier—whether you simply sense ground under your feet, the flavour of a cup of coffee or the warmth of your own bed—these are just as relevant as any perceptions you may begin to get of other dimensions.

The 'sight' is basically extremely commonsensical and practical, and you need to remember this. Far too many people imagine quite mistakenly that it involves a complete withdrawal into 'other' worlds, constant states of trance and being entirely unable to live comfortably in the world of the physical. But one of the most important lessons 'sight' actually teaches us is the necessity for balance, for everything to be utterly and uniquely its own self yet form an integral part of the whole.

NO WRONGS, JUST SHADES OF RIGHT

One of the most common misconceptions is that possessors of 'second sight', or indeed any kind of psychic ability, must be godless individuals who lack moral standards. In some ways this could be said to be true, but it is also very far from the truth.

If you are going to develop your potential for 'second sight' you will certainly not have to give up any belief in God nor even renounce your own particular church. But you will need to be prepared to widen the scope of your awareness to include the 'rightness' of all other forms of faith and to lay aside dogmatic assertions that only your own way is the 'right' one.

If you see with the 'Sight', you see that ALL IS AS IT SHOULD BE. And that includes awarenesses that may appear to conflict with one particular creed, though how—or even whether—specific religion fits into this picture is something for each person to work out for himself. But since there are no boundaries confining what the 'Sight' may reveal, all forms of human faith, or even the lack of faith, have a place.

The 'sight' encompasses everything without judging it, wanting to set it to rights, 'educate' itor otherwise revise it in any image of what the human ego thinks it should look like.

When the boundaries of judgement are lifted so also are the boundaries of 'moral standards' as society normally defines them, since the 'Sight' does not look with human eyes or apply human rules (whether these are considered to be 'moral' or 'civilised' or not). It does not judge or administer punishments or reprimands. The language in which it speaks, the language of prediction, prophecy or simple reportage of what it sees, is detached and without personal bias, so far as this can be achieved and maintained.

Logically, this might well sound like a recipe for complete chaos, universal licentiousness and irresponsibility, and it is no wonder that a distorted, partial or uninformed view can provoke stirrings of panic. In actual fact, though, awareness of the 'Sight' involves the lifting of other, more subtle boundaries too; and when these are removed so is the need for, and temptation to indulge in, the kind of selfish, irresponsible behaviour usually regarded as resulting in licentiousness, chaos, godlessness and an abandoning of 'moral standards'.

When you possess the 'Sight' you see that just as there is no judgement to be made there is no blame or guilt either. We create our own blame and guilt, sin and shame as well as that of others, in attempting to cover up the deficiencies in ourselves rather than accepting them. For if we do accept them, we accept that AT THIS MOMENT they too are AS THEY SHOULD BE.

Just as the wisdom of the 'Sight' does not work according to rules of cause and effect we might normally try to apply, neither does its appreciation of the rightness of things work according to the rules of any particular applied 'religion'. Religions largely teach that we try to improve ourselves (and others), to live a good life and love our fellow men with the aim of pleasing God or becoming more like him. The 'sight' gives a subtler insight into the nature of each soul's ultimate responsibility for itself. It sees that attempts to progress along the path of spiritual advancement and wisdom must be made because the way, the potentiality for development, is there rather than because this course will gain approval. Increasing maturity and the advancement of the spirit is its own achievement, not a measuring by some end result. And since every stage is equally necessary, equally a part of the soul's progress, all is as it should be at any given instant.

Rather than thinking of the soul's journey as chronological, starting at a 'beginning' and proceeding to an 'end', it makes more sense to consider its nature as circular. Therefore apparent beginnings and endings—like concepts of 'better', 'higher', 'further'—simply become points on the circle. We are all at different points but since we are not in competition we are all in our different ways progressing equally well. Some souls may be more aware than others it is true, but this does not mean they are 'better'. All, whatever point they have reached, are equally achieving, their efforts equally important and valuable.

With this awareness comes a maturity of thought and attitude. 'Seeing' with the 'Sight' does not involve acquiring but letting go, not a shoring up of defences, a feverish attempt to build up material and emotional securities but a realisation that there is no need for them, no need to fear. And it is fear that lies at the root of the chaos and irresponsibility—and all that springs so distressingly from them.

But fear of what, specifically? The answer is that second sight sees only the truth and most people are very frightened by absolute truth.

SEEING TRUE

The behaviour most of us are taught in western society involves looking the other way, covering up, pretence because we feel we are not doing what we rightfully should be doing, or not trying hard enough. All these express themselves in a lack of openness and honesty.

If you can 'see' and accept the truth of situations then you do not need to make excuses, blame others, become a control freak, manipulate in order to get your own way or absolve yourself from guilt. And if you can not only 'see' the truth but speak of what you see in the only language that will describe it, you need never resort to playing word games, indulging in one-upmanship, fearing that people will misunderstand you, trying to soften the blow, worrying in case you have made a fool of yourself, or created a bad impression.

All of these are behavioural patterns of the immature, the uncertain and fearful whose boundaries are very limited. The fact that they are also the behavioural patterns of politics and most social interaction in the world today should provide food for thought.

The person with second sight, or who is making a serious attempt to cultivate his innate ability, must be prepared to give up all forms of dishonesty, evasion and deceit. He must not be afraid to try constantly and sincerely to free himself from guile, and to avoid any kind of behaviour that is based on anything other than complete truth, both with regard to himself and others.

Many would-be spiritual people are only too

eager to vow at this point that they will never tell a lie again. Some even protest in indignant outrage that they have always been completely honest in the past. But they probably have no conception at all of what real truth entails and it is far from easy.

If you 'see' the truth of everything, and speak of what you see, you must be prepared, for instance, to think twice before indulging in uninformed speculation or gossip: you must avoid giving any kind of false impression by flirting or casual behaviour. You must be ready, if this is the truth of the matter, to admit without rancour that you have made a mistake or that you are wrong; and to refrain from passing judgement on anyone else's beliefs, opinions, behaviour, values or ideas. And yet you must be ready to state truthfully all you may perceive or want to express yourself.

In our modern society, such behaviour is practically impossible to maintain. However, your awareness of the 'Sight' will mean you will begin to set yourself these kinds of standards because you want to adhere to them. For the same reason you will try always to keep as near to your truth as you can.

So far as rules of behaviour are concerned, you will become increasingly aware of a natural rightness of things in which compassion and considerations for all are paramount, where distorted motives and hidden agendas are revealed to the eyes of the 'Sight' and have no place. There are actually no rules as such, for as we have seen, boundaries of any kind do not exist when seeing with the second sight. Some visionaries have, however, attempted to convey what they perceive as true ways to live in their work, whether painting, music or literature.

Consider the following lines from William Blake's AUGURIES OF INNOCENCE:

To see a world in a Grain of Sand
And a Heaven in a Wild Flower,
Hold Infinity in the palm of your hand
And Eternity in an hour.

A Robin Red breast in a Cage
Puts all Heaven in a Rage . . .

A dog starv'd at his Master's Gate
Predicts the ruin of the State.
A Horse misus'd upon the Road
Calls to Heaven for Human blood.
Each outcry of the hunted Hare
A fibre from the Brain does tear.
A Skylark wounded in the wing,
A Cherubim does cease to sing . . .

56

A truth that's told with bad intent
Beats all the Lies you can invent.
It is right it should be so;
Man was made for Joy & Woe;
And when this we rightly know
Thro' the World we safely go.

All creative and artistic people possess second sight to some degree and all products of their creativity are an attempt to communicate what they see with their own particular vision. There may be immense wisdom in what such people intuitively perceive, and often they can open up new visions to others or act as a catalyst for such awareness.

But because of their strong sense of artistic identity, creative artists are inclined to delude themselves and however powerful their vision or message, it is important to remember yet another revelation of true second sight. With all boundaries removed, you cannot even be sure that someone else's truth and reality will be the same as your own. And this too is AS IT SHOULD BE. In the end, only you must be responsible for yourself, your own clarity of vision and your own sense of what is true and has to be.

THE COMPANY YOU KEEP

The developing child moves from the company of toddlers to that of pre-teens, then teenagers, and finally into the adult world. Similarly the development of second sight and the growth of spiritual maturity will also mean that the individual's needs regarding the company in which he feels at ease will change.

Without in any way passing judgement on anyone, it is nevertheless true that a person who can 'see' beyond the words that are spoken and whose realities include dimensions beyond the material, will find conversation with some people so limited as to be almost impossible. The 'sighted' person will be increasingly inclined to avoid the company of those whose values and preoccupations are lacking in any spiritual element, or based on distortions of truth as the 'Sight' perceives it.

There is nothing superior or arrogant about this. We all pass along the same path but have reached different points in the journey. And the 'Sight' recognises the relevance and necessity of ALL the stages of growth and progress, making no distinction between the beginning and the end. ALL IS AS IT SHOULD BE. There is no 'right' or 'wrong' place—but understanding between those at different stages is necessarily limited.

People who begin to develop spiritual/psychic awareness and to trust and use their 'second sight' will inevitably find that they begin to view at least some of the people around them in a different light. They often find, however reluctantly, that changes have to be made in the company that, for their own spiritual progress and peace, they need to keep.

As we have seen, the possessor of the 'Sight' is more often than not slightly suspect to his fellows, and especially if he attempts to explain his new philosophy of life, will probably be derided for his attempts to 'be honest' about what he sees and says. Later, he may feel that others consider him slightly embarrassing or uncomfortable to have around.

The attitudes of others are, however, something that they, not you, need to come to terms with. You may not be able to change the world, and other people's perceptions need to be respected, but you can consciously choose what you are prepared to accept into your own heart and mind. If you set standards high for yourself, you can also refuse to settle for less than the highest standards in those around you—even if you find as a result that (temporarily at least) you are spending your time alone.

But being able to 'see' the whole truth, and choosing to face it and accept it, does not necessarily mean that others must be forced to do the same. One of the most common queries I encounter regarding 'second sight' is whether whatever is 'seen' should always be revealed in full. 'If you see something upsetting, like the loss of a child, or a person's death, what do you do then? Especially since you claim you must never tell anything but the truth.'

This is the sort of question that worries many enquirers. Is there ever a time when a white lie or some kind of gloss-over and pretence is justified? Or does the full and brutal truth always have to be told?

The answer is as subtle as each individual case. You yourself may be aware and ready to accept the truth but as we have seen, many people are extremely frightened by it. And however far you might have proceeded along the path of awareness yourself, you must respect the fact that others have different standards, are at a different point along the path, or may not even value awareness at all. Many people are not ready or able to face the truth in its entirely: equally, though, it is not up to you to judge when they have progressed far enough. This is the kind of dilemma that only a skilled seer can attempt to resolve.

Often, others will surprise you, and though you could do a great deal of harm by trying to force truths on to those who cannot take them, you must allow others the freedom to decide what they will accept at any given time. Here is once again a paradox: you should not reveal all, yet you must withhold nothing. Each individual must be given every opportunity to progress and grow and it is not for you, or anyone else, to decide when or how they are to do it. The decision is for them alone.

Consequently, as a rough working rule, one offers only what seems appropriate to the situation and the moment but should be ready to reveal more if asked. If traumatic events or personal tragedies seem inevitable, you do not necessarily need to inform the individuals concerned that they are about to die or that their son will be involved in a car crash and will be paralysed. You look at other aspects of the truth you can offer instead—and there are always positive aspects. You may tell the enquirer who seems to be close to death, for instance, that he or she will be much happier by the time a year has passed and that the grinding difficulties of the present will have been resolved satisfactorily.

If you 'see' an accident in the family, you might perhaps phrase your prediction that the ups and downs of domestic life will cause the family to grow closer and become more positive and supportive of each other. There is no need to give finite details though always, if the person can take it, it is best to make no easy promises. You could, for instance, say that though there are trying times ahead you can see that the person concerned is strong and brave enough to tackle them and that he/she will come through the experience a wiser and better person.

Even if the event (like a death) seems inescapable, it is best not to try and force it onto the person concerned unless they ask outright. If they do it is probably because they know intuitively what is going to happen and they may not be looking for fairy tales about how everything will be 'all right' but for respect for their attempts to face the truth as best they can without flinching. Second sight can offer reassurances that death is not the end, that there are other worlds and other ways than the physical.

But even then, the strength and power of other people's realities may be able to turn the potential future into quite a different actuality. And there are always miracles. You very rarely need to bend the truth even a little, but use your own judgement and experience to give what seems appropriate to the time, situation and individual.

LOOKING SIDEWAYS

When you are ready to remove the barriers and suspend judgement and you have allowed your mind to wander through prospects of thought that give you a sense of the limitlessness of the 'Sight', you will begin to receive messages/ visions/inspirations or whatever you like to call them, that will give you glimpses of the truth of things.

These may come in any way at all—as intuitions, signs, omens, seemingly coincidental or synchronistic mention of names or words, thoughts, ideas. You will probably be inclined at first to doubt them and yourself. You will find they come, as it were, sideways rather than obviously ahead of you so that you can recognise them. You will also find you experience the 'Sight' as a kind of inner certainty, a conviction that has been granted without your being aware of it.

Through daily meditation you will begin to learn that the 'Sight' involves spiritual discipline. Random and uncontrolled 'sightings' will probably start to occur. It is at this point in their development that many people feel the need to begin consciously working with one of the formal, recognised tools that make it easier to focus the vision.

*   *   *

OPEN YOUR EYES: SESSION NOTES

All spiritual development, all forms of psychic and extraordinary power, require the disciplines of on-going practice. It is not easy to be able to let go of other distractions so that you can start to open deliberate communication with other planes of existence, other worlds.

Whether or not you really believe there are other worlds at this stage does not matter. Learning how to relax will be beneficial in any case, since achieving relaxation and mental discipline helps to alleviate stress and make for a healthier and happier lifestyle. So these are some basic guidelines following on what we have discussed in this chapter.

1   Put aside a few moments every day to devote to conscious development of whatever spiritual/extraordinary abilities you possess. Start with perhaps ten or fifteen minutes and extend the time to suit yourself. Make sure that for those few moments you will be quite alone and will not be disturbed by anyone or anything including phones, doorbells, pets or other members of the household.

2   Sit quietly in an upright chair with your hands loosely resting on your lap and your feet together. Do not cross legs or ankles. The reasons for this are so that you are grounded and conscious of the physical—the earth beneath your feet—as well as aware of the spiritual, and so that the natural energies circulating in the body are able to flow freely. Some authorities advise also removing watches, rings and anything tight that could impede the energy flow but there is no rigid rule and a good guide is always to do what you think feels right to you.

3   If you prefer to lie down you may do so, but take care that you do not make yourself so comfortable you drift off to sleep.

4   You may like to burn some incense or a scented candle and play quiet music consisting more of rhythm than melody, chant or natural sounds rather than words. The reason why candle flames, scents or chant-type sounds are associated with 'seeing' is not some spooky secret, it is simply because they assist the senses to let go of conscious every-day awareness. Scents soothe and uplift, a rhythm or chant releases the mind from consideration of musical form and (as we will see later)

helps in promoting a state of heightened awareness.

5   You are not likely to encounter anything that will upset or frighten you as the whole process of relaxation and meditation is intended to promote peace, tranquillity and well-being. Nevertheless as at all times when you are dealing with other planes and other worlds, it is wise to say a prayer before you begin to some source you feel you can call on to bless your undertaking and protect you in what you are doing. This might be God, Allah, the Goddess or any other higher power that is positive and enlightened. You may also like to keep a symbolic sign of the seriousness of your spiritual quest near you or wear it round your neck—a cross, crucifix, ankh, Star of David or something similar, whatever you genuinely believe in as good and holy.

6   There are two components involved in letting go of tension which you will need to become aware of and consciously practise during your periods of meditation. They are breathing and physical relaxation (which induces mental calm). There are excellent cassette tapes available from most New Age or Mind/Body/Spirit promoters that will give

you detailed step by step instruction on relaxation and breathing control. Invest in one and if you would like to explore the subject further, consult a book on Yoga breathing or better still, take a Yoga course. Yoga breathing is not quite the same as the deep breathing you will be taught in relaxation exercises but all or any of these methods of relaxation and breath control will help you in your everyday meditation.

7   The aim of relaxation exercises is to teach you how to be able to relax the body completely at will. This is done through familiarising you with the process of relaxing each of the muscle groups of the body in turn. As a beginner, however, before you have been taught about relaxation and breath control, simply try to be comfortable and breathe deeply to the bottom of your lungs a few times, shrugging your shoulders to relieve tension.

8   Relaxed and breathing easily, begin to open your mind for your ten minutes of practical meditation and simply let your thoughts drift. Natural sounds—running water, the sea—or a drum rhythm or chant may help, or if you wish, keep silent. Aim at emptying your mind completely of

any thoughts at all, perhaps by imagining you are gazing inwardly at a huge black velvet curtain. You will find this impossible at first but keep trying, and whatever thoughts creep in, simply move them quietly out again.

9   There are exercises you can learn from books—or from practical work in a Development Circle—which will help develop your psychic abilities. Looking fixedly into a candle flame, for instance, or concentrating your mind and consciously willing something to happen—perhaps for a particular person to phone you. But as we have seen, second sight is not concerned with making things happen so it will be enough simply to relax, open your mind and wait.

10   Tapes of what are called 'controlled' or 'guided' meditation are available to guide your thoughts, and these may be useful if you cannot concentrate on your own. But ultimately, your second sight will not need guidance and it is better if you can train yourself to focus your mind yourself.

11   At the periphery of your vision, or on the furthest edge of your hearing—just within the boundaries of awareness—you will begin to 'see', 'hear', or 'know' images or

thoughts which have come to you via 'other' sight. They may be tiny, even superficial or apparently ridiculous. Take them, examine them, put them aside. Do not attempt to make sense of them or try to prove whether they are true. Simply examine them and let them go.

12 When your ten minutes or so is up, consciously close your mind to your 'other' sight until your next meditation session. Make a short prayer of thanks for what has been granted to you (even if you seem to have achieved nothing) and return to the every-day world.

CHAPTER 4

FINDING THE RIGHT TOOLS

When you begin to work consciously with the 'Sight', expanding your mental horizons and becoming aware of extraordinary sensations, it can feel disorientating at first. The practical and the philosophical aspects of 'seeing' do not appear to be related and their respective realities can seem impossibly far apart.

Do not worry about this, simply enjoy being alive and aware, able to accept yourself and what you are doing. Simply BE. Knowing that all is well—all is as it should be—is just as much of a spiritual discipline as making weighty efforts to divine the far reaches of space and time. As I have already mentioned, any kind of mastery in this field cannot be achieved overnight.

Setting aside a regular meditation or study period each day, deliberately devoting time to your psychic/spiritual development, will bring the reality of your gift into clearer focus and make it part of your everyday life. If you are going to be able to work with it, this has to be done in complete acceptance since the gift will to some degree be with you all the time. You cannot just assume it when you feel like being 'sighted' and be like everyone else when this seems more convenient.

There are responsibilities attached to the gift of 'Sight'. You must be fully aware that second sight is a way of life, that you cannot see-saw between the values, standards and insights it bestows and other visions of reality. You may be able to perceive that others do this, and why they do it, and since there are no rules you will always have free choice over the position you decide to take. But because the vision is always constant and what is revealed is uncompromisingly clear, you will never be able to delude yourself about the truth.

We have seen that at this point many people feel they would benefit from an applied discipline and are glad to begin working with something physical. This can keep you on course and steady as you find your feet in very different mental environments. There are various methods available, but broadly—apart from studying the formal systems such as Astrology, Graphology and Numerology, which have their own rules—the possessor of second sight trains himself to work with the gift in three main ways.

1   Using some kind of focusing tool (which can also include the formal systems mentioned above).

2   Through trance and altered states of consciousness, including the dream state.

3   By release from the body and going into other realms and dimensions.

WORKING WITH FOCUSING TOOLS

Using some kind of tool to assist concentration of the inner vision is the most common method of attempting any kind of divination or enlightenment. Since second sight is simply an awareness that involves no spells or working of magic, it is the vision itself that matters but especially when beginning this kind of work, a tool can aid clarity and precision as well as accuracy.

The tools most commonly used for 'seeing' and divination are:

TAROT CARDS (or any other types of cards)
RUNES (including various kinds of Rune Stones, Rune cards, etc)
CRYSTALS (including crystal balls)
THE BOOK OF CHANGES (I Ching)
BONES, DICE (or other objects for throwing or casting)
SAND/COLOURS/WATER (and other less

popular methods of divination in the West)

Any objects that may be used for divination—whether Tarot cards, Rune stones, crystal ball, yarrow stalks or coins used in working with the I Ching—have no power in themselves. Crystals are charged with their own personal energy, but none of the objects can divine or work any kind of magic. The cards are just squares of printed or painted board, the stones and crystals are inanimate pieces of rock, however beautifully polished or worked, and the yarrow stalks remain just yarrow stalks.

Even when they are used most effectively, none of the tools themselves actually alter. The vision, the power that sees with the 'Sight' may be stimulated by these traditional, often ancient tools but it can never transform them or imbue them with independent power. The uninitiated have always found it difficult to differentiate between the tools used and the power itself, however, and claims are still made that Tarot cards, for instance, are wicked or dangerous. Even today they can provoke over-reaction in those who see them although this can work either way—they may even be regarded as potential miracle-workers instead of distasteful or threatening.

Both of these extreme views are wrong. The

tools that can be used to work with second sight and enhance its effectiveness are purely a means to an end, even though all of them are steeped in the significance and tradition of their own impressive histories. But by themselves they can do nothing, either harmful or good. It is only if used by a person possessing the 'Sight' that the objects employed to concentrate it can be activated.

THE TAROT CARDS

The Tarot pack as we know it today consists of seventy-eight cards. Fifty-six of them make up what is called the Minor Arcana—four suits similar to ordinary playing cards. The suits in the Tarot pack are of Swords, Wands (also known as Staves or Rods), Cups, and Pentacles (also known traditionally as Coins). They are numbered from one (the Ace) through to ten, with four additional 'Court cards'—Page (in some modern packs Princess), Knight (or Prince), Queen and King. The Latin word 'arca' meant a box where secrets could be hidden, and like the term 'arcane', the term 'Arcana' means 'secret' or 'mysterious'.

The other twenty-two cards of the Tarot pack form the powerful Major Arcana. Each carries a picture and each is named and numbered (at least, modern cards are named and numbered, though the earliest cards carried nothing but painted images). It is possible to work with the Major Arcana alone or with the whole pack, and some practitioners prefer to use more than one Tarot pack for a reading.

Nobody knows the actual history of the Tarot or where the cards originated. Neither does anyone know definitively exactly what they mean. All that can be claimed for certain is that they have been used in some form from very ancient times—playing cards have roots in Chinese, Indian and other eastern cultures. They entered Europe probably during the Moorish occupation of Spain, though claims have been made that it was the returning Crusaders and the nomadic Romany or 'Gypsy' races who were responsible for introducing them to the West. The Tarot cards, in an early form, were used in mediaeval Italy in a popular game called 'Tarocchi'.

The earliest Tarot cards in existence date from the fourteenth century. Sixty-seven cards still survive (in varying locations) from a pack supposedly painted for Filippo Maria Visconti, the Duke of Milan, though it appears that this pack became mixed up at some stage with other packs painted later for the Visconti and Sforza families. One was by an artist called Bonifacio Bembo and there is a modern pack based on these beautiful Renaissance pictures with their rich blues, reds, greens and gold which is known as the Visconti-Sforza (or Bembo) deck.

Two other popular and familiar packs are called the Waite or 'Rider' deck, and the Tarot de Marseilles.

The original source for the content and imagery of the cards has variously been claimed to be Ancient Egypt, Ancient Celtic mythology, and the Hebrew Kabbalah among others. But because the physical Tarot is actually nothing more than a series of images and symbolic pictures, it is possible for almost anyone to design a Tarot pack. Some traditions even advise working, if you are serious about reading the Tarot, with your own cards, which you can draw or paint yourself.

So long as the traditional symbols on the cards are roughly the same, or at least represented in intent and thought, the pack will prove just as effective as any commercial one. Some years ago I tried creating one for my own use (the Major Arcana only) which consisted of ordinary photographs of family and friends selected carefully from my junk-box of old snapshots, mounted and laminated. It might have lacked the detail and finish of professionally designed Tarot packs, but it worked.

The pictures and images on the cards are considered to hold a complete picture-language with its own mysterious symbolism and deep occult significance that can be understood only by the initiate. One tradition even has it that the reason why the cards originated was because prophets and seers possessing the 'Sight' were often regarded with suspicion. They and their knowledge suffered persecution and periodic 'cleansing' by the less spiritually aware, and their hard-won wisdom was in danger of being lost. Pictures contained hidden meanings and teachings that could be 'read' by novices coming fresh to the spiritual in later generations were the answer. And so, it is said, the traditions of the cards evolved.

There are many excellent books on the Tarot and its meaning and significance, giving most of the traditional methods of reading the cards. You can even attend Tarot schools and get direct tuition or learn from tapes or postal courses. This book is concerned with the Tarot only as it relates to 'second sight'.

As with Astrology, Graphology and other formal methods of divination, Tarot too has its 'spreads'. These can be used to do a reading even by those with limited intuitive vision and probably the most popular one is called the Celtic Cross. Books crammed with detailed and specific interpretative information will tell you the traditional significance of each card and the significance of their relations to each other in a 'spread'. Subtler works will inform you of the mysteries of the Tarot as a guide to spiritual life and the progress of the soul.

Second sight uses all and none of these methods, since each time a card is consulted with the 'Sight' in different situations and for different people, it might well have an entirely different meaning. By concentrating on the images and allowing whatever comes to present itself into your mind, you can learn to use your 'Sight' to obtain information that might well have come anyway without the assistance of the cards, but which presents itself in a clearer, sharper form and much quicker.

Any other packs of cards—such as playing cards, 'Oracles', 'Psy-Cards', even 'Rune Cards' or the many modern kinds of designer decks—will work the same way for the possessor of the 'Sight'. The images are only a catalyst for the vision itself, a trigger as it were which, when touched, causes the explosion to happen. The psychological tests known as Rorschach inkblots and others work on the same principle by opening up the mind to what is generally called 'free association'. But with the 'Sight' one works to take the vision much further.

THE RUNES

Similar in tradition to the Tarot, but with their own fascinating and powerful history rooted deeply in the mists of the north, the Runes too are the outward manifestations of an ancient, mysterious and secret language. The Runes were—and still are—used not only to allow messages and enlightenment from gods and ancestral spirits to be given by the seer (in the past, some shaman or priestess of the kind called a 'Volva') while in a state of trance, but to actually facilitate shamanic journeying into other worlds.

As with the Tarot, there are excellent books available providing background to the history of the Runes and explaining how these series of cryptic signs and symbols originated and developed among the ancient Germanic and Celtic tribes. The Runes exist in several different forms: as the unspoken mysteries they represent; as the signs themselves, traditionally carved or painted on pieces of wood or stone; and as their sounds, the 'names' by which they are referred to. The caster of the Runes is aware, however intuitively, of all of these. And when they are cast it is not to 'look into the future' as such, but to consider the over-all meaning and significance of everything, the cosmic patterns represented by the patterns of nature, the cycles and seasons, ebbs and flows of eternal existence.

CRYSTALS

The traditional image of a 'fortune teller' always peers into the future by means of a crystal ball, but when you look into the crystal what do you see? The answer is nothing, not with your physical eyes. There is nothing there except the crystal itself.

But scrying, crystal-gazing, looking into a pool of water or a mirror—some of the most ancient methods of divination—have been practised since the beginning of time. The principle by which they work is the same as that of the 'shining object' a hypnotist will hold up in order to help his sitter relax and enter the trance state. Whereas water or reflected light cannot be touched and handled physically, however, crystals and other precious and semi-precious stones provide seemingly solid objects that can be used to 'hold on' to what lies beyond them.

Since the dawn of history, jewels and gems have been regarded as precious, though ancient man was probably not as aware as the physicists of today of the nature of matter, and the scientific fact that all things vibrate (as Fritjof Capra puts it) in 'rhythmic patterns . . . determined by molecular atomic and nuclear structures'. The particular properties of gems and crystals—their coolness to the touch, their attributed powers to heal, cure, assist and enlighten—may be accounted for in this way by scientific fact, rather than mere fictional fantasy.

The Greeks named the crystal from their *crystallos* (frozen water). Greek legend has it that truth existed as a crystal and that Hercules dropped the gem when he was climbing Mount Olympus. The crystal shattered, scattering tiny fragments throughout the world.

Crystals and other stones, rocks and gems are all formed in a natural evolutionary process within the earth's crust. Their values are only those man has placed on them, all have their own particular beauty and properties. There is no true 'precious' stone— all are precious in their own right. A piece of coal which can fuel the warmth of a fire could, if allowed to continue evolving long enough, eventually help to form part of a diamond.

Gem stones have always been recognised as sources of spiritual truth and power. The ancient High Priest of Israel, for instance, communicated with the God of his people through secret instruments called the 'Urim' and the 'Thummin'. The bag in which these oracles were contained was worn on the breast and studded with gems specified by God himself, even their names a veritable treasury of splendour and magnificence. They include emerald, topaz, sapphire, diamond, beryl, onyx, jasper, agate and amethyst.

Crystals need not necessarily be of clear quartz, the 'frozen water' or ice of legend. The 'rose quartz' is a beautiful pink colour and bestows a sense of wellbeing, self-love and confidence. Other clear quartz may contain traces of any colour at all, or be almost any colour. If you personally find the thought of working with crystals interests or stimulates you, there are excellent reference books to help you become familiar with this secret and fascinating world.

Possessing or using a crystal or crystals to assist your gift of second sight will bestow calmness, detachment and wisdom.

THE I Ching
The tiles of the ancient Chinese game of Mah Jong, have been used for centuries for divination and have sometimes been regarded as a kind of eastern counterpart to the Tarot and western playing card decks. They are not in such common use today though they were very fashionable in the earlier years of the nineteenth century in western society, when the game was an accepted social pastime like

Bridge or Whist. The Chinese traditional method of divination more likely to interest the beginner (and about which popular books of instruction and interpretation are available) is the I Ching, the Chinese Book of Changes.

Unlike the cards, and more in the way of the Runes or crystals, the I Ching does not specifically answer questions or reveal the future, rather, it links in to the eternal ebb and flow of all existence, the principles of balance and harmony, the concept on which it is based being the complementary opposites yang and yin, which correspond to all other concepts of compementary polarities—Good/Evil, Light/ Dark, male/female and so on. What consultations of this ancient text will reveal to the enquirer are the moments when times are ripe or inopportune, whether to wait or to go forward, whether the 'changes' and the forces that are current will work for or against plans and actions, and what methods of behaviour are best suited to the times. This gives the enquirer a guide to how to best 'go with the flow', to make use of opportunity when it is there, and avoid wasting valuable energy, worry and effort when the time is not right.

Of course, it is far more subtle and complex than that. The ancient oracular teachings are once again expressed in mysterious symbols, image pictures that are open to subtleties of interpretation. They express themselves in the very language of prophecy and potentiality— the ACTUAL and POTENTIAL futures co-existing and waiting, shifting worlds, layers of reality which need to be investigated and discovered by the questioning soul on its spiritual quest.

The secret language of the I Ching consists of sixty-four hexagrams (six-line diagrams) each with its own meaning. In the west we are most familiar with the hexagrams through books that describe them (in English) and add interpretations and commentaries—the best known is the Wilhelm version.

The method of consulting the oracle is traditionally by using fifty long yarrow stalks. The process takes time and concentration, the stalks have to be cast but the ritual must be carried out in order to obtain the numbers necessary to make up the lines of the relevant hexagram, which will provide insight into the question or problem that is being considered. The number of permutations of the lines of the hexagrams allow for no less than 11,520 possible answers, so the depth and complexity of this source of wisdom is virtually inexhaustible.

Beginners or students in the west do not usually use yarrow stalks but prefer to cast coins—often round Chinese cash coins with holes in the centre which provide a physical (or mental) link with Chinese tradition. In fact any coins that are identifiably two-headed with an obverse and reverse image may be used. Three of them are needed for casting, and they should be about the size and weight of at least a two-pence piece, as experience reveals that smaller and lighter coins may not fall cleanly enough and if one of the throws is doubtful, the procedure should be begun again.

Though the results obtained from casting the coins do actually produce a definite answer—one of the hexagrams—the messages themselves allow for intuitive 'Sight'. But because this system is subtle and complex and the hexagrams are not perhaps as visually suggestive as a picture on a painted card—as well as the fact that the established rituals need a certain amount of time to perform them, most beginners find the I Ching difficult.

IN GENERAL

Of all the various tools and instruments that have been used for divination, the Tarot cards, Runes, crystals and the I Ching are the ones in most common use in the west today. However, throwing or casting is a method that some people find suits them and you could well find you get results from objects such as dice or bones. Real bones (which I have seen some western practitioners use) can appear rather gruesome and smack more of the determined shaman or 'medicine man' rather than simple second sight. But every person has his or her own way and if you are intended to use bones in order to 'see', that is what you will need to do.

Sand, colours or water are sometimes used for divination, as are objects in the shape of a ball or an egg. A ball is like a ring, the symbol of eternity, and an egg is similarly regarded as a symbol of cyclical renewal and rebirth, the true secret of life.

It is customary to keep cards, crystal and so on wrapped in a cloth, traditionally of silk, or in some lovely and ornate box. The only reason for this is as a mark of respect, not because they will not work otherwise or will deteriorate. Your tools and instruments for 'seeing' must be treated with proper appreciation of their qualities, but you should value them as an extension of your spiritual self, for their role in helping you find truth and wisdom, not for their own sake. As we have already noted, they have no power in themselves.

When you have begun to feel at ease with

whatever tool you have chosen to work with, and when the time has come for you to start applying what you 'see', you will sense it. Though instruction can be given on how to develop second sight, you must begin as soon as you sense you are ready. Have confidence in your own awareness of rightness and truth and act on it without asking permission from anyone else. A 'sighted' person is at once his own master and teacher, as well as an eternal novice and student. This is another paradox which will make itself apparent to you.

Follow your intuition. The best indication of whether you are going the 'right' or the 'wrong' way is in how it feels to you. If simple, natural and spiritually truthful all is well. When you find things getting complicated, when the human ego and the brain begin to intrude, forcing decisions and alternatives upon you, you probably need to think again.

FINDING THE RIGHT TOOLS: SESSION NOTES

When you begin to work with any kind of focusing tool you will need first to simply become used to its presence, to spend time just handling, examining or merely having near you your cards, crystal or whatever you have chosen to assist you in developing your second sight.

As to the choice of tool, you will find that if you consciously decide to use the cards, say, or crystals because you like the idea of being able to reel off complicated predictions that refer to 'The Wheel of Fortune', 'The Tower Struck by Lightning', 'The Lovers', 'The Hermit', 'The Devil', or you think a crystal will look mysterious and impressive, you will probably find it hard work to get anywhere at all or feel any affinity with these particular tools. Your way of working, whatever it is to be, will choose you, rather than the other way round.

Remember that the spiritual directive is always to BE rather than DO. Even trying to cling to control by making conscious choices in this respect is to defeat the object.

In the case of any kind of spiritual progress, you will find everything will come to you if you simply open yourself to it and wait. Ways will open, directions will be given, all will be made absolutely clear if you simply let it happen. Even the choice of a crystal or jewel to wear around your neck or on your finger must be left to the stone itself to reveal itself as yours.

When choosing any stone, jewel or crystal, or deciding on a set of Runes or pack of cards, prepare yourself beforehand with a short prayer or meditation, asking to be guided wisely. And before you choose spend some time just looking at whatever selection is before you.

You may have thought you would like an amethyst, for instance, since its imperial purple denotes power and influence—but the particular stone you need will draw you towards it and that is the one you must choose even if, rather disappointingly, it turns out to be a rather nondescript piece of agate. The balancing and general harmonious properties of the more humble agate will almost certainly be what you need at that particular moment, perhaps to actively discourage you from becoming too ambitious in the obtaining of power and influence.

It will probably be a while before you find your own particular way, your own instrument, which works best for you. You might also discover that you need to explore different cultural beliefs and systems before you become certain of your own spiritual identity.

Some people feel drawn to the traditions of the East, to the ancient Vedic or Chinese beliefs or to the Tibetan or Buddhist faiths. Many become fascinated by the rich spiritual culture of the Native American Indians or the Celtic tradition. Do not be afraid to investigate all beliefs that draw you, for there is something to be learned from them all. As we have seen though, true second sight does not confine itself within formal boundaries. It encompasses all—and nothing. In the end, the 'Sight' will guide each individual in his or her own best way.

1   Your first steps in wisdom and spiritual discipline are to learn how to slow down, to let go of even the need to obtain answers at all.

2   During your regular meditation periods, continue to work on your relaxation and breathing exercises, allowing yourself to handle your cards, crystal or whatever but making no attempt to try to 'see' anything. If any sensations or visions do come, examine them as before and put them aside. We have noted earlier that getting visions is relatively easy—almost anyone can learn to do it. It is learning to control and discipline the gift that is the difficult part.

3   At this stage perhaps more than any other, it is important that you consciously dedicate your endeavours to the source of light and goodness, to God or whatever you perceive to be pure and holy. It must be emphasised again that you are unlikely to encounter anything that will frighten or harm you but the very willingness to

believe and trust can sometimes, in those inexperienced in working on a spiritual/psychic level, leave them open to unpleasant experiences. This is not a game: all spiritual development must be undertaken with the utmost seriousness.

4 Be aware of the need to protect yourself, and familiarise yourself with methods by which you can do this. A basic prayer, a protective symbol, will probably be more than enough but as you progress in sensitivity you will need to avoid picking up negativity that is not your own. A simple protective device is to imagine you are standing under a twenty-litre tin of white paint, which is being up-ended over you. Consciously visualise the white liquid covering every part of you—hair, skin, clothes, even beneath your feet—and then use your 'skin-suit' of light to deflect anything dark and negative that is thrown at you as you pass through the day. An alternative method is to imagine you are stepping into a white 'radiation suit' complete with protective face-visor, and picture enclosing yourself entirely within it.

5 You might feel you are making no progress but the gift of 'Sight' is similar to the gift of an operatic voice and an

important part of the training is NOT to use it at certain times, allowing it time to develop. You need at first to allow the physical body to learn to interact with the mind. Relaxing and learning control over physical functions like breathing, frees your mind and spirit and gives it scope to exercise its abilities without hindrance.

6   Constantly remind yourself just to BE instead of busily trying to DO all kinds of workings-out, exercises or readings-up about second sight. The meshes of the physical and the spiritual will engage of their own accord with no effort on your part.

7   Be aware all the time of the need to remove boundaries and judgmental attitudes from your mental horizon. You will find they continue to creep in despite your best intentions. And if you found the philosophical quotations in the previous chapter rather boring and skipped them, go back now and read them again. It is by opening your mind to such words and thoughts even if you do not understand them, that you will begin to work out truths and realities for yourself.

8   Here are a few more comments to consider about the nature of the 'Sight'

and how it views things. These are not from recognised philosophers but from ordinary people I have encountered in the course of my work. All three are 'second-sighted' to varying degrees and are attempting to pursue a spiritual path.

'It's a kind of intuitive knowledge and you don't learn it. You're just sort of, well, put in touch with it, like being tuned in to a certain wave-length, and the messages, the meanings, come through in images or impulses in a sort of code. You repeat the code, even if you don't really understand what the message is all about. But there's always—always—this certainty, a complete and utter certainty of truth.'
JANINE B.

'It depends how you view good and bad health. When you look at it this way, you know there can't possibly be any state of health at all in living that isn't in some way useful, significant or necessary to the over-all rightness of the whole. Sometimes though, it is difficult to see straight away what it is, but speaking for myself, when I look back now, I can see that everything I have suffered in my life has been there for a reason.'
PERCY ST. J. (aged 83)

'I used to feel angry and upset because things weren't right with the world, but I didn't think I could do anything about them. But I have seen

that simply by refusing to condone or allow them into my reality, and standing up honestly for what I will or not accept, I make a step forward along the path. And though all my efforts to prevent outrages and social injustices like cruelty to animals or children seem as ineffectual as a few drops of water in a huge ocean, I try not to despair about it but to concentrate on my own steps forward.

'If everybody in the world just took one step, it would alter the world for everybody.'
STELLA M.

CHAPTER 5

STATES OF ALTERED CONSCIOUSNESS

Most of the prophetic, visionary or inspirational messages that are passed on by individual seers of whatever kind, involve some state of altered consciousness—particularly the trance and dream states.

Trance is defined by my pocket dictionary as 'a state of suspended consciousness'. This may be spontaneous or self-induced and ranges from the momentary 'day dream' or mind wandering familiar to everyone, through the light hypnotic trance that aids relaxation, to extreme states of frenzy and ecstasy brought on by drumming, chanting and the use of alcohol or drugs. It might also be considered to broadly encompass clinical conditions such as epilepsy and the various mental disorders in which consciousness of reality is suspended.

Though we all pass in and out of trance states to some degree during the course of everyday living, the deliberate cultivation of a state of suspended consciousness—in which we are extremely open and vulnerable—should not be undertaken lightly or treated as a game. Newcomers to circles in which psychic

97

powers are developed under supervision are warned to be careful. They are made aware that they might let in energies that, while perhaps not harmful in themselves, will feed on any negative emotions. It is in this kind of way that hysteria and uncontrolled behaviour can develop and as we have already seen, powers like second sight bring with them the responsibility of learning to control them through intense spiritual and mental discipline.

It was long believed that individuals who could induce trance or even, like sufferers from epilepsy, entered the state spontaneously, had been 'touched by the gods'. When the priestess, the Pythia, who was the Oracle of Apollo at Delphi, sat 'in the smoke' and passed into trance, the god was considered to have spoken through her as though he had actually occupied her body and been present himself in person.

The summoning of gods—known as Theurgy—was a solemn act. The priest or priestess who acted as the mouthpiece of the divinity was required to prepare by fasting and meditating for long periods before entering the trance state, and was sometimes kept apart from enquirers in case contact with them proved too real and caused the entranced person harm. Questions had to be put through yet another intermediary.

When acting as any kind of spiritual medium—the word means 'way' or 'channel'— the physical body becomes suspended, is held immobile and unaware between life and death. Therefore it is no melodramatic invention that in some circumstances sudden noise or light or any violent recall might be very uncomfortable, to say the least. Accounts of seances in which spirits were contacted have often contained hair-raising details of mediums being shocked into death by attempts to expose them and their trance states as fraudulent.

Trance can certainly be faked to some extent and there have been cases where stage magicians or other con merchants have tried to gain from exploiting the credulous and the bereaved. Nevertheless trance states are perfectly authentic and respectable and are increasingly being recognised in forms of hypnosis and self-hypnosis, to aid in self-help therapy and healthy, stress-free living.

Many psychically gifted people will tell you that when they go into a trance state, they receive messages or enlightenment from entities described as 'Spirit Guides'. In a state of trance, conscious awareness is partial or non-existent and the way is cleared for other awarenesses to make themselves manifest: individuals speaking while in trance may have no conscious memory of having done so and at the time have no control over what they say. They may, however, be aware of communicating with beings—familiar or unknown to them. Whether they are really communicating with some deity, a soul that has passed beyond the grave or a 'Spirit Guide', even whether these beings represent the individual's Higher Self or repressed emotions, guilts and fears, is not part of the second sight as such and therefore does not concern us here.

TRANCE

Working with a focusing tool like the Tarot cards is one of the easiest ways to induce a state in which conscious awareness is suspended. While concentrating, the individual narrows and deepens his awareness to such an extent that he will not notice what is going on around him, or even within himself. Bodily discomfort, hunger, thirst and tiredness remain unacknowledged until he has finished what he is doing. This trance-like state occurs in many other contexts during creative or artistic work. Actors enter it once the curtain has risen, authors experience it when they sit cramped at their desk for hours, lost in what they are writing. Composers and painters are all familiar with it.

Intense concentration fixes the mind and frees the body. It is a state that is highly pleasurable and can become addictive. And the more the mechanisms that induce trance are practised, the easier it becomes to enter the trance state and, in whatever way, use it positively.

The lines between so-called madness, the visions of genius, the revelations of religious ecstasy and the awareness brought by second sight are often difficult to identify, particularly by people who have little experience of any of them. Even those who directly experience states of trance are generally unable to describe them except in the vaguest of terms, and cannot explain what happens or how it works.

There are many levels of trance, and though trained hypnotists are aware of the depths of trance into which they are able to put those who consult them, most people have no idea of when they actually begin to enter a trance state or of what to expect. It is generally believed that those in trance black out completely and have no consciousness of what happens around them, what is said to them, or what they might say or do themselves. The fact that shamans, 'medicine men', even Sufis such as 'Whirling Dervishes' all appear to invoke the trance state through convulsions, spinning, leaping or frenzied activity, seems to underline this. Consciousness of the real world has, it seems, to be completely lost.

It is this aspect of trance, of course, that has been seized on by 'stage' hypnotists. Their acts typically consist of persuading individuals from the audience to perform activities they would find highly embarrassing in their conscious state, but which cause the audience a good deal of amusement—perhaps behaving as though they are six years old, or they are dancing with the Bolshoi.

In fact, in many cases of induced trance consciousness is not necessarily lost to this extent and there may well be an overlap between the outer reality and the inner perception. Many people who have experienced spontaneous entrancing, undergone hypnosis to help them give up smoking, say—or even within my own experience, been relaxed enough to regress to the far past in connection with this or some previous life—may feel they were not actually entranced at all. All the time they were aware of their surroundings and did not actually 'black out' for the duration of the session.

Even though trance does not necessarily entail 'blacking out', some awareness of the passing of time or the actual details of normal living will be lost. But altered consciousness, or even suspended consciousness, is by no means the same thing as unconsciousness.

The human brain, incredible instrument that it is, limits our ability to see, know and understand as fully as we might simply because it is part of our physical existence. It allows us to perceive everything but limits our interpretation by sorting what we experience into categories to help us survive in the physical world. Within our experience, it tells us what is possible—and what is impossible.

Trance is the means by which we not only push the possibilities of human existence to its furthest boundaries but are also able to enter the world of the impossible. Second sight is actually no more than the ability to do this in reverse—to recognise the world of the impossible as not only possible but the true reality, and to have to make a conscious effort to limit ourselves within the accepted and imposed boundaries of human rational thought.

The trance state is actually far more common and more pervasive than most people realise. All car drivers are familiar with driving from one place to another perfectly efficiently but on 'automatic pilot' as it were, so that they cannot remember anything of the journey. This state was once described in a court case involving a charge of reckless driving as 'highway hypnosis'. Sportsmen and women can reach incredible peaks of achievement while in a state of complete detachment from their physical selves. In fact any type of concentrated studying or creative work can induce trance and with regard to endeavour, whether artistic or otherwise, this actually makes sense for it is more than an act of will to attempt anything.

The breaking of an athletic record might, rationally, not appear to be physically possible; writing a novel of a hundred thousand words that attempts to give meaning to the full range of human experience—these are acts we might never undertake if we were in our 'right mind'. In other words, if we were limited by conventional human thinking, we would never realistically undertake them. A performance of MACBETH, the execution of a painting, the composition of a symphony all pose this same dynamic. Creative acts as well as feats of bodily endurance and prowess are more than physical exercises of the human will—they are nothing less than acts of faith.

The composition of poetry illustrates how this process works: the poet, traditionally, is seized by his (or her) inspiration or 'Muse', which he perceives as something outside himself. He allows the Muse to possess him, existing throughout the process of composition in a 'world of his own' apart from the real world. He feels compelled to record his poem while the inspiration is present, before it leaves him. And what is even more interesting is that afterwards, he invariably feels what has been revealed to him—what he has been privileged to create in his exalted state—is intensely meaningful. He is compelled to share it with everyone else whether they want to participate in the experience or not.

By consciously cultivating the Muse, regardless of what he imagines it to be, the poet is in the same position as a diviner or seer. For the creative process involves nothing more than the ability to perform self-hypnosis (sometimes spontaneously, sometimes through practice) in order to enter the trance state to some degree. Those who work unconscious of what they are doing will tell you that they cannot call the Muse, they have to wait for inspiration to arrive. But like all students of the spiritual, serious creators—professional writers who have to work to a deadline, for instance—learn this is not the case.

The state commonly known as 'waiting for inspiration' can be controlled and the creative trance induced quite matter-of-factly, with no magical intervention involved. Like any kind of mental or spiritual discipline though, this involves effort that the 'occasional poet' or even the 'weekend shaman' may not be inclined to want to apply.

It is not easy to master and cannot be achieved overnight. But once entranced, the subject will find that the impossible moves tantalisingly within reach. All forms of beautiful art can be created, and physical fears of mind-boggling wonder can be achieved.

Many records exist of literary or other artistic works that 'came' to the creator as a result of somehow placing him or herself into a state of trance and most commonly, such states were achieved through the use of some form of drug. It is no mere coincidence that a great many geniuses, as well as those who never made the grade, have lived their lives in states of almost constant trance as opium eaters, smokers of hashish or addicts of some similar substance, including psychedelics such as LSD—anything that artificially expands the boundaries of reality.

Most creative people have tremendous intuitive second sight but artists do not generally find it easy to achieve the detachment that is necessary for working with the 'Sight'. Because of their personal involvement in what they do, they are inclined to want to create patterns of their own instead of accepting the cosmic picture as it is revealed to them. True seeing, as we have noted, brings not only the vision itself but also the wisdom to know what that is seen must be accepted as it is without the ego presuming to interpret it in ways humanity thinks will make better sense. Most creative people have large egos—and they are reluctant to relinquish them.

INDUCING TRANCE

Relaxation, controlled breathing and focusing the mind all help to induce the trance state. Concentration on some object may assist—and candle flame or crystal symbolises all the objects that seers of the past gazed intently upon before they were able to make their divinatory pronouncements. Traditionally, hypnotists swing some glittering object before the eyes of sitters with suggestions such as: 'You are feeling very sleepy . . . your eyelids are growing heavier and heavier . . . now they are closing . . .' But it is actually quite easy to induce a trance state without any swinging object and the voice alone can have the same effect if the sitter is suggestible.

Cases have been recorded in the East of holy men or magicians who could induce such deep and complete states of trance that they could survive for long periods of time—

sometimes, it was claimed, even years—entombed in sealed coffins or boxes in states of 'living death'. One such case recorded in the CALCUTTA MEDICAL TIMES in the early 1830s concerned an Indian fakir called Haridas, who in a strictly supervised experiment was buried in a sealed chest for forty days before being dug up again apparently clinically dead. He was, however, successfully revived within an hour.

Entertainers like Harry Houdini, seeing the immense potential such feats held for enhancing their status as professional conjurors or illusionists, have successfully duplicated many seemingly miraculous exploits but their achievements have largely directed attention away from the original truth of the matter. The question of how the feat is done is what now fascinates the public, rather than why such things were undertaken in the first place.

Specifically, the trance state has always been regarded as the way in which wise and enlightened counsel, as well as omens and divinatory signs, not readily available in the consciously state may be obtained. It should not be an end in itself and indeed is of little or no use if regarded as such—some kind of quick fix to popular entertainment or a cop-out from the responsibilities of living that consciousness brings, a way to avoid all the pains and problems of living in this world.

Spending your lifetime learning how to enter a physical state of catatonic 'death' and passing months entombed in a coffin might even appear to be defeating the object, but this particular spiritual path, as well as any other, can be right for some if undertaken in sincere and questing humility.

It is difficult for a mind reared in one culture to comprehend the disciplines of others, but the sources of wisdom have no allegiance to any one 'right' continent, country or creed. There have been—and probably still are—other methods of inducing trance that can seem equally bizarre to those not accustomed to them. Fakirs prepared themselves for their long state of suspended animation by sealing off their orifices and some of the inner passages of the body in ways similar perhaps to those mastered by dedicated athletes. They also included extreme forms of fasting and yogic cleansing of the organs of the body prior to entering into the trance state.

Ancient civilisations like that of the early Celts encouraged a state of altered consciousness in warriors before a battle. The wild frenzy that struck such fear into their enemies was called 'furor'. And followers of the Norse god Odin, too, entered a similarly frenzied state, which gives us the modern term 'going berserk'.

Often these states were achieved to the accompaniment of blood-letting as well as the more usual chanting, drumming and dancing. The Celtic shaman passed into trance after an animal had been ritually slaughtered and skinned. He would wrap himself in the still-steaming pelt before suspending his conscious awareness in order to prophesy, communicate with the gods and spirits (notably of the animal kingdom) and pass into the Otherworlds. Followers of other religions—for example the Sufi, an Islamic mystical sect—let go awareness and blurred reality through frenzied dancing and violent whirling that blotted out any familiar or coherent sensation.

'Magic mushrooms', mescalin and chemically produced psychedelic hallucinogenics like LSD have traditionally been used in rituals to loosen the bonds of normal consciousness and induce altered states of awareness. But true second sight actually needs none of these things. It is achieved through control of the will and discipline of the mind. The effort of learning to control the 'Sight' is a necessary part of the vision itself. Shortcuts to wisdom do not happen.

THE CASE OF CAYCE

One of the most notable psychics, prophets and healers of recent times—if not indeed of all time—was born on a Kentucky farm on 18 March, 1877. Edgar Cayce has been described as the 'Sleeping Prophet'. During the course of his life he gave thousands of what he called 'life readings' and readings requested by patients to diagnose and treat (or heal) physical ailments but he knew nothing of what he said, for all his consultations were carried out in a state of complete trance.

The transcripts of many of Cayce's readings are archived at the Association for Research and Enlightenment (founded by Cayce) at Virginia Beach in the United States. He is particularly notable for his remarkable record as a healer, only needing to be told the name and address of the sick person after he had put himself into trance, before he was able to make a diagnosis of their complaint and provide the remedy. This he would give in explicit medical language, with directions not only of substances to be used in treatment, but the treatment itself. Treatments were sometimes extremely unorthodox but the accuracy of Cayce's diagnoses and the percentage of well-documented, proven cures he effected is remarkable.

In addition to his healing, his life readings and prophecies explored all the great mysteries of life and death, past, present and future, and abound with wisdom and truth. Even sceptics have been unable to deny that the man himself (who died in 1945) was of unimpeachable integrity, a sincere and exceptional human being. He did not profit from his work and for the greater part of his life remained poor. His death was brought about by overwork and stress as a result of giving too many readings to help victims of the Second World War.

What is particularly interesting to us about Cayce is that he left accounts of the methods he used to induce the trance state. Though they were intuitive and he could not rationally explain them, they nevertheless reflect many similar accounts from other sources.

Cayce would first loosen any restrictions to 'free-flowing circulation' around his body—shoelaces, belt and so on. We noted earlier that many authorities prescribe similar actions, including uncrossing ankles, feet, arms and hands so that the spiritual energy is able to pass in, through and then out of the physical body during the trance state.

Cayce reported that he would next lie down on the couch in his office. If he was about to undertake a 'physical' (a healing) reading he lay with his head towards the south and feet towards the north; if it was a 'life' reading, the opposite way about. He said he did not know why he had to do this, but the information in the readings calls it 'polarization'. This concept is in fact reflected in other systems and cultures—and compare the principles of Feng Shui, for instance, where placement of objects is paramount.

Next Cayce said, he would place his hands on his forehead between and slightly above the eyebrows 'on the spot where observers have told me that the third eye is located' and pray. The third eye, one of the chakras or energy centres of the body, is regarded as the gateway to spiritual enlightenment. This is also, by ancient tradition, the location of the 'eye' that sees with other or second sight. Often clairvoyant people will press the position of the third eye on the forehead when working with their 'Sight'—this is, of course, the age-old gesture of 'looking for inspiration'.

Cayce described how he would then wait for a few minutes, 'until I receive what might be called the "go signal"—a flash of brilliant white light, sometimes tending towards the golden in colour.' This light, he said, was the sign that he had made contact. If he did not see it, he could not give the reading. Such flashes of light, colours or shadowy glimpses on the periphery of your vision can be the first indication that you are receiving messages—being able to 'see' with your second sight. (But do visit an optician if you suspect you have eye trouble.) You will soon learn to recognise the difference between purely physical symptoms and manifestations of the extraordinary, and they may occur not only with your vision but in the realm of other senses as well.

Next Cayce described how, after seeing the light, he moved both hands down to rest on the solar plexus. (Actually another of the chakras.) Though he himself was by then unaware of it, his breathing was noticed by observers to become increasingly deep, rhythmical and from the diaphragm. This kind of deep breathing is often evident in the trance state.

After several minutes of lying with glazed, though open eyes, Cayce's eyelids would slowly close and the assistant (generally his wife Gertrude) knew he was ready to be given the information he needed. If it was a 'physical' reading this would be the name and address of the person requiring the reading; or the name and date of birth if it was a 'life' reading. He would then begin to speak.

'I am entirely unconscious throughout the whole procedure,' Cayce reported and added:

'When I wake up, I feel as if I had slept a little bit too long. And frequently I feel slightly hungry—just hungry enough for a cracker and a glass of milk, perhaps.'

This may reassure those who wonder how, and in what sort of state, individuals return or 'wake up' from trance. In most cases there is no problem, though hypnotic trances should not be induced in other people if the hypnotist does not know exactly what he is doing. A person under hypnosis will generally wake quite easily and painlessly when instructed to do so, and even if he does not respond immediately, further calm and repeated instructions will achieve the desired effect. Horror stories of souls 'lost' or 'trapped' in the trance state are just that—tales bandied about by the uninformed.

For those who want to learn to induce trance themselves it is usually recommended that, in the beginning at least, there is a friend present so that if they get into any difficulty they will not be alone. But I have never come across anyone within my own experience who 'got into difficulties' if they carefully followed the basic safeguards we have mentioned—a preliminary prayer for guidance and protection, a sincere intention of spiritual questing, a determination to hold fast to the light in selflessness and detachment. Problems are only likely to arise if the person concerned is undertaking his psychic development for the wrong reasons—personal gain or power, greed or a desire for some selfish and negative motive like revenge. And even then he is not likely to get 'lost' or 'trapped' in trance.

If you induce the trance state yourself, you are in control of your own mind and can wake yourself whenever you want to by exerting the power of your own will. You will soon become accustomed to doing this with practice. Or, if you really doubt your abilities, instruct a friend to use a form of recall to awaken you until you have the confidence to 'bring yourself back'.

Edgar Cayce was a deeply religious man, a Christian believer who read through the entire Bible each year of his adult life. By 1933 he had read it, he said, fifty-six times. He believed in the power of prayer, and that his gifts were from God, given him in order to help others. Nevertheless he did not attribute the readings that were given through him while in trance unequivocally to the 'voice of God'. He was of the opinion that the wisdom and knowledge revealed came from his ability to 'tap' the universal records, made up not only from the subconscious of each individual as it passes through time, but the collective records of all previous (and possibly future) existence. Such sources have been described generally as 'race memory'; Jung called them the 'collective unconscious'; while more esoteric authorities refer to them as the Akashic records.

'Apparently,' Cayce reported, 'I am one of the few who can lay aside their own personalities sufficiently to allow their souls to make this attunement to this universal source of knowledge—but . . . really and truly, I do not believe there is a single individual who doesn't possess this same ability I have.

'I am certain,' he added, 'that all human beings have much greater powers than they are ever conscious of—if they would only be willing to pay the price of detachment from self-interest that it takes to develop those abilities.' And these words underline all that we have already noted about second sight.

DREAMS AND DREAMING
In spite of experiments and years of theorising, we do not really know what happens in our dreams. The sleep and dream states have been identified by scientists as necessary to our health and well-being. Without being able to sleep we would die, and it has been proven that without being able to dream, the mind would not be able to function effectively. Torturers have long been aware of the potential of depriving the body of sleep, though it was not understood until

comparatively recently how sleep itself worked and how dreaming occurred.

Yet in spite of all our knowledge, the dream-state is still beyond our control. Though the dreamer is still present in physical form within a sleeping body, he is manifestly 'not there' so far as communication is concerned. The state of death, which is far more drastic, can be overcome when or if contact is made with the spirits of the departed, but dreamers are never available for questioning.

So is the dream-state a kind of 'half-death' where the dreamer is neither in the world of the living or the dead? Is it some type of trance? Or something quite different?

From earliest history dreams have been regarded as deeply significant. Ancient civilisations practised the art of Oneiromancy, divining the future from dreams. Ancient writings—such as the Bible—are filled with accounts of dreams and their interpretations. The popular press never stops informing the general public how to understand and translate the mysterious symbolism of dreams while even psychiatry itself, the 'science of the mind', has its own classic works on the subject, from Freud's INTERPRETATION OF DREAMS and Jung's MEMORIES, DREAMS AND

REFLECTIONS to more modern investigations.

There have been many theories about the nature of dreams, and if you are interested you will be able to find innumerable books on the subject. It has been argued that dreams are reflections of our hidden fears and problems in symbolic form, that the dream-state allows a kind of 'acting out' of potential different solutions. Another theory is that the brain, like a giant computer, needs to 'process' our short-term memory before the impressions it has absorbed during the course of a day's living can be 'down-loaded' for permanent storage in its long-term memory banks. This last theory makes a lot of sense in my view and as a matter of interest, if you examine your dreams carefully you will find that almost every component in each night's dreaming will relate somehow to your physical awareness during the past twenty-four to forty-eight hours.

We could speculate for ever, but no-one really known for certain exactly how our dreams work or what they are for. Most of them seem to be quite meaningless, trivial and irrelevant—they might tell psychologists a good deal about us but they do not appear to hold any real kind of import or significance. Intuitively, though, we are aware as people have always been throughout history that in some way our dreams are vitally meaningful, that they do give us messages. Like prediction and prophecy, they speak in their own language and it is one the rational brain cannot understand. This is a specialised area for 'seeing', but if you do feel drawn to dreams and dreaming there are reputable books to start you on your way to working with, and learning how to become familiar, with that shadowy twilight world.

In the course of many years working with psychic and second-sighted individuals, I have never encountered a single one who claimed to be primarily a 'dream diviner' or similar.

And so far as 'seeing' is concerned, most impressions are received in the half-way state between waking and sleeping. Whatever processes the subconscious mind initiates while the body is asleep, their meanings are likely to be too surreal and foreign when presented in the forms of dreams themselves. In the half-awake-half-asleep stage, however, meanings are often given in crystal-clear words or awareness we can understand, and it is this kind of enlightenment that prompts people to remark: 'I woke up and my mind had sorted it all out in the night'.

In fact much more than simply sorting out problems can be achieved while in this altered state of consciousness. It is ideal for working with the 'Sight' and in fact most people do it all the time, though quite unconsciously and with no real appreciation of the power they are exercising. The answer to a problem may seem so obvious—and such a blessing—that it is seized on with relief; but with other impressions or messages that swim into the half-awake consciousness, the rational brain will be inclined to intervene. Our human limitations are once again likely to get in the way of simply accepting what we may perceive with 'Sight'. Again, it is very necessary to simply take what we are given on trust and in faith.

Some dreams are of course unmistakably prophetic, and these have to be placed in a class of their own. The normal surrealities we may experience in a night cannot be compared to instances such as those reported, for example, previous to the Aberfan disaster when a Welsh school was destroyed with great loss of life. One person dreamed that the name ABERFAN was being spelled out in vivid light, another that large numbers of schoolchildren in Welsh national costume were going to heaven. The disaster that did occur was completely unforeseen and the people who experienced these and other such dreams lived in different parts of the country and had no connection with Aberfan.

We have to accept that when this kind of

dream occurs there is something present beyond mere spiritual truth or enlightenment, but so far as second sight goes, there is really no explanation to seek. We have seen that the 'Sight' operates by laws of its own, so all we need to know is that by whatever means, some flash of knowledge from future time has been able to make its way into present awareness. The 'Sight', being outside of time as we perceive it, is able to 'pre-call' as well as 'recall' happenings and events.

ALTERED STATES OF CONSCIOUSNESS: SESSION NOTES

Once accustomed to the idea of mental/spiritual discipline as part of your everyday routine, having begun to familiarise yourself with inducing and working with trance, you will discover you become aware with your 'Sight' automatically. Messages/ visions/revelations will come in their own way, however, and you need to be able to recognise the forms they take—whether thoughts or knowledge that just 'comes into your head', images and pictures within your inner vision or something else that is personal to you.

1   Remember that the 'seeing' is far more important than anything you may want to 'do' about what you see. Learn to restrain yourself from rushing off to put your new awareness of truth and wisdom to immediate use.

2   The novice always wants to enlighten others, to change the world overnight. Remind yourself that ALL IS AS IT SHOULD BE and that perhaps you might do more harm than good by assuming you know what is best for everyone else.

3   Remember that you need to cultivate the quality of complete detachment. You cannot help others by assuming their problems and pain, by deciding you will carry their burdens for them. What you 'see' will almost certainly be coloured to some extent by human emotions, whether your own or those of someone else, and you must be constantly aware of this. Only a complete detachment from desires, needs, pity and other human prompting, will leave your vision truly clear so that you can see what is really there.

4   When 'looking' on behalf of others, you may find that what you see will be a reflection of their own hopes, desires and wishes rather than what is truly there for

them. Only experience and practice will equip you to identify such subtleties of interpretation.

5   You must, at the same time as being aware of pitfalls such as the ones above, have complete confidence in your own power of 'Sight' and speak—when you are ready to do so—with authority. Give only what you see, exactly as you see it, using your sense of judgement about how much of the truth to reveal. You may offer an interpretation but make it clear that it is only your suggestion, not fact. Do not give more than you see or make guesses. If you cannot see what is asked for, say so.

6   Never be drawn into argument or defensive discussion about what your vision reveals. It is up to those who consult you whether they accept what you might tell them or not. It is not up to you to try and force your vision on anyone. Remember that the 'Sight' encompasses ALL—and NOTHING. Their reality may be quite different to yours. Respect their truth as you acknowledge your own.

7   Find the best method of 'seeing' for you. Try, for instance, practising automatic writing or 'channelling', holding a pen or pencil in your hand and opening up your

mind to see what 'comes through'.

8   Keep a record of your spiritual/psychic/visionary progress as honestly and exhaustively as you can. When you doubt yourself or your abilities—or even the reality of second sight itself—which you certainly will from time to time, refer back to your 'diary'. Note down as you go any quotes, sayings, inspirational thoughts—whether your own or from some other source—to revive you when your confidence is low.

9   Remember that you are your own teacher as well as seeker after truth. In a spiritual/psychic/visionary sense YOU ARE ON YOUR OWN. No-one can ever be aware of your own personal reality except yourself.

CHAPTER 6

OUT OF BODY

Most people becoming aware of their 'second sight' find it enough to apply themselves to learning how to achieve trance, familiarise themselves with the methods by which they can 'see' into other times and places and make connections with sources of enlightenment and wisdom (whatever these are perceived to be). Many who begin to consciously and seriously cultivate their extraordinary abilities may well in a relatively short space of time become active and practising diviners, psychic advisers or whatever else they may choose to call themselves and enter into a whole new way of living. But when it comes to proceeding further, to progressing beyond 'seeing' and trance and being prepared to act as a channel for messages, inspirational wisdom and/or prophetic enlightenment—what then?

Many are called perhaps, as the Bible so succinctly informs us, but few are chosen-whether as shaman, 'medicine' or other 'wise man/woman', priest/priestess, or whatever other term is applied to it. The average possessor of 'second sight' is unlikely to want or need to pursue this path consciously, at least in the beginning. And with all the best intentions—or lack of them—in the world, it is impossible to know who will eventually emerge as one of the chosen. As with all spiritual matters, you do not choose WHAT YOU WILL BECOME. You are allowed in due course to discover WHAT YOU ALREADY ARE and can choose either to accept the calling or not.

For those who do discover that this is the way they are to go, it is here that the true learning process really begins. Whatever wisdom and mastery they may have achieved, however disciplined they have become in working with their second sight and spiritual/psychic gifts, all who reach this point are made aware that, though they might have regarded their strivings (perhaps over long years) as an apprenticeship to earn their place at the top of the mountain, they have in fact only been trudging along the track that has brought them to the lowest foothills.

Practical guides abound on subjects like how to perform 'astral projection'; how to become familiar, and communicate, with the animal kingdom; how to 'leave the body' in sleep and/or confront the phantoms of your imagining in the shadowy territory of your dreams. All these touch on the third method we have mentioned of working with your 'second sight': bypassing intermediaries and going to the sources yourself; assuming the mantle of the adept, the shaman or speaker for the people, direct representative of this world. It means you are willing not just to open your consciousness to outside sources and act as a channel for communication, but to actually set aside your physical self when it is necessary to do so, to proceed into other realms, planes and dimensions.

Though the idea can sound quite like fun, the realities of what is involved generally prove to be far beyond the abilities—or the needs— of the average individual. Those who are chosen, however, will be required to work at learning how to separate their spirit and their body and gain mastery over both. They will be required to lay aside all they thought they had achieved; to see and acknowledge that far from reaching the top of the mountain, far from having become a master, they must now in complete submission assume, mentally and spiritually, the saffron robe of the novice, the lowest and humblest seeker after truth.

This way is not for all, and the average individual need not bother his head about such matters. If he is not one of the chosen, it will mean nothing to him. If he is, and when he is called, he will know about it.

INITIATION AND THE SHAMANIC JOURNEY

Extremely wise and enlightened people of all cultures have always known, however intuitively, that the way of spiritual maturity is not easy. It need not necessarily be so painful for everyone, for we can choose how far and how fast we travel.

Beyond being able to 'see' into the future and understand something of the wider concepts of existence, suspending as far as possible all human attachments and reactions that blur and obscure the vision, the serious student must undergo a spiritual initiation into the Mysteries. He must suffer the symbolic 'death' of his human self in an initiatory process that may take years before he is then 'reborn', purged and purified—albeit still for the moment within a human body. He must undertake a journey—and again the image is a symbolic one, though in some cases individuals do actually tramp across continents or undertake pilgrimages to some far place as a seeker for truth.

In most cases, the novice does not know what he is seeking, nor what he will find, and he will have no guarantee that there is actually anything to find. The spiritual process of initiation into the Mysteries—in whatever form—has to be taken blindfolded, completely alone, entirely in faith, though it might not be clear where that faith should be placed or even whether there is really anywhere at all to place it.

Before the truth can be found, it must first be lost. Before the wise man can truly discover how to know and be aware, he must have lost the ability to see and the awareness of everything. This is the real paradox at the heart of the 'Sight', higher wisdom and teaching revealing that all that was most valued must be sacrificed in order that it might be truly seen for what it was—nothing in the face of true worth.

Once you accept your 'Sight' and adjust your outlook accordingly, you are already on your way to leaving behind for ever all the indulgences, desires, needs and childishness that make up the realities of our physical existence. But it is because this life can seem so enjoyable, so sensually and physically good, that few people are willing to consider 'giving it all up' for the sake of some elevated spiritual concept.

Whether they have the capacity to do it is another matter. The capacity is always there for everyone and potentially, we could all take the way of the shaman, the novice in his saffron robe, walking fearlessly into

Otherworlds. But most are not willing—even if they are able—to perceive that the choice is there.

This kind of choice is not conscious, it is made on a deep internal level and the responsibilities it brings are awesome. Again, futures like this are ALREADY DECIDED, and if they are to be we cannot alter them. But it is up to us when we are ready to make the choice.

'You may see yourself as a child struggling along a long hard road and not getting very far,' counselled one great source of enlightenment, 'but look around you and be comforted. Many have not yet reached the road.'

HOW IS IT DONE?

No-one can ever know what happens to the spirit while the body is entranced or its equivalent. We can discover the physical symptoms—that the pulse rate and breathing can slow down so much that life appears to be suspended, and that like a hibernating animal an individual in trance can sometimes exist for long periods without the basic requirements of life. We can observe and test the physical symptoms but this is as far as it goes. It is not possible to test what happens to the soul and/or the mind. The only evidence we have is what the individual tells us when normal consciousness returns.

Often, this is unhelpful. Because mental and physical activity takes place outside the reality most people accept, it is impossible to describe it in terms that the person with no experience of such things can relate to. But of course, there have been those who, undeterred, have tried to fill in the details.

When we speak of going 'out of body' this is naturally a mental concept. No part of the physical being—no pieces of flesh or bone—can actually leave the entranced body and then return to it. It is the soul or spirit that 'goes out' of the body and then comes back again, and how this is done is difficult to grasp. Scientists, as we have noted much earlier in this book, have yet to be convinced with hard evidence they recognise, that it can be done at all.

Experiments have been done over the years to try and establish such matters as the weight of the soul. One doctor carried out tests with tuberculosis sufferers in the early part of the twentieth century, weighing them (in their beds, bed and all) while they were alive and later, after they died. The difference in weight, he argued, would tell him what the 'life essence' that had departed from the body measured in physical terms—but the results were inconclusive since the difference in weight before and after death was only a fraction of an ounce, extremely difficult to determine.

In fact the soul, the 'life' that comes and goes out of the flesh as we are born and die, cannot be measured. It exists on a different plane of being. And the way in which someone in trance may go 'out of the body' is equally quite different to their getting up and walking out of the door. The other worlds into which they may proceed are also mental concepts rather than planets or other 'real' worlds like this one.

There have been notable accounts, often with step-by-step instructions, by individuals who have spontaneously (or after much practice) mastered the ability to 'leave the body'. The abilities of religious masters are far beyond the scope of the average person but men such as the American Robert A. Monroe, who in 1972 published his JOURNEYS OUT OF THE BODY, might be no different to ourselves. According to his book, he was 'living a reasonably normal life with a reasonably normal family' when in 1958 he began to experience 'manifestations' that allowed him to experience 'Out of Body Experiences' (OOBEs). He found he was able to 'leave' his physical body, 'travel' to other areas of the United States and 'see' things happening there on which he was able to report when he 'returned'. Being a journalist he was aware of the necessity for objective reporting of his experiences, and he submitted himself to various tests under laboratory conditions. Others have written from varying standpoints of belief about OOBEs, and whether they have regarded their travels as within an 'astral' or some other kind of body, it is up to the reader to make what he will of these accounts.

'Second sight', as always, remains silent about what it 'sees'. And though it seems a fascinating idea to be able to whirl off around the globe, to view things happening elsewhere with whatever advantages this might involve, does it actually matter whether one can perform such acts? The same question applies to feats like being buried alive for months. What, in the end, does all this accomplish?

Again the clue lies in BEING, NOT DOING. Regardless of what methods are involved, what explanations are given, what experiments are carried out and proof obtained (or not), all the 'Sight' is concerned about is 'seeing'. The vision of the truth simply IS, and there is no need to DO anything.

The traditional image of the hermit or holy

man represents the most concentrated and advanced spirituality generally evident in one who simply IS, living quietly apart; he does not 'socialise', achieves nothing the world recognises, and offers no political answers or theological creeds. The greater the spiritual power, the less 'doing' there has to be. And perhaps this explains why experiments involving psychic ability, testing telepathy and clairvoyance are often unsuccessful. The truly powerful have no need to put themselves to the test or prove anything.

INTO OTHER WORLDS

Practices of the adepts of all cultures, stories of the great hero figures of myth and other such archetypal inspirers of humankind, all reflect the concepts we have just mentioned. All deal with advanced wisdom and transport the initiate, whether in person or vicariously, into realms where the human foot cannot rightfully tread. The symbols of initiation; the symptomatic 'death' of the personality in order that the soul may be reborn in its more advanced and purified state; the tradition of the 'quest' or 'journey'—all of these appear over and over again in the legends of the past.

It is when we view these aspects of existence with the 'Sight' we begin to see what part the dark side, the suffering and pain, must play in keeping balance between all things. This is a concept difficult to grasp except in fragments and sudden visions. But if the spiritual path is so difficult, so filled with testing and anguish, with torments and trials, we might well wonder what kind of personality will consciously choose to follow it and even consider the rest well lost for the sake of what it offers. Some kind of masochistic, sacrificial skivvy who does not know how to enjoy living is the popular view.

But viewed with the 'Sight', enjoyment takes on a different form from the one we normally imagine to be ideal—no problems, no pressure; time to sit and bask in the sunshine; romance, wine and good food, all the pleasures of the physical. For those with the 'Sight', appreciation of all these is actually heightened since true awareness of the physical becomes fully possible—but at the same time, none of it matters. The spiritual and the physical are different; and the 'Sight' has the same relationship to the physical as great literature has to ABC and 'The cat sat on the mat.' It forms a necessary foundation for what may eventually be achieved but that is all.

From personal trial, the willingness to accept and overcome pain and suffering, the spirit emerges refined, cleansed and purged. Like the particles that constantly dance in their sub-atomic shifting of matter, nothing stands still. It must move one way or another, and it is growth, stretching, reaching in all directions and achieving transcendence and transformation, that holds the stamp of what is AS IT SHOULD BE in the revelation of the 'Sight'.

Heroes of all times, and places, are the representatives of mankind's intuitive aspiring. These mythical characters were generally beings with very human faults and failings, but they were willing to dare the dark shadows of the worlds of the Dead, the Underworld, the Otherworld, far-flung empires beyond the stars, even the realms of the gods. Of course, being human they generally needed some assistance to be able to make these epic journeys, and more often than not they undertook these quests for all the wrong reasons—but they went. By their willingness to endure, or if necessary perish, they returned having acquired the beginnings of wisdom and a greater awareness of truth.

PAIN, SUFFERING AND EVIL

A word more is perhaps necessary on the subject of pain, suffering and evil. The fact that the 'Sight' accepts everything with extreme detachment and does not interfere or judge, can give rise to the impression that it will not only shrug and look the other way at problems of pain, suffering and evil but actually condone them.

'If you say that everything is as it should be, then pain and suffering is acceptable and right, is that what you mean? And evil, cruelty and horrors like that, are they to be permitted and dismissed as right too?'

It might seem so, but the 'Sight' is always paradoxical and the answer to angry questions like the ones above are far more subtle and complex than either a direct yes or no. In fact, the answer is both yes and no—and neither yes nor no.

Everyone, at some time in their lives, will experience suffering and pain, whether mental, emotional or physical. That is a fact of existence and cannot be altered. No amount of second sight will change it, since we are all human beings living in physical bodies in a physical world. In fact 'sighted' people can be badly affected by the suffering of others since they 'pick it up' and feel it physically or mentally themselves: this is one of the reasons why they need to learn to 'switch off' and be able to protect themselves. While the 'Sight' increases an awareness of the suffering of others, it also provides the means to learn to cope more effectively with your own.

We are all human beings. We have to accept that we are never going to understand anything lying literally beyond our understanding— which has to include any kind of cosmic or divine plan, the reasons why we are here, or what life, living and dying is all about. And so we have to look at suffering, face it in all its awfulness and accept it. But with 'second sight', we begin to see that it is only a part of the whole, one aspect of the full picture. The 'Sight' reveals that 'wellness' and 'illness', pain and suffering as opposed to the absence of pain and suffering, are two sides of the same coin.

Second sight underlines the truth evident in the teachings of most religions, that there is a right (here meaning 'rightful' rather than morally correct) time for everything. All is as it should be at this moment, but it could very well be quite different when we think again, though we need to discipline ourselves: be aware of what might need to be done, but leave the doing—or not doing—to the individual concerned.

Everyone must pass along his own learning path and be responsible first of all for himself. We may regret, even shed tears, that those we love—or even complete strangers—are having such a hard time and do not seem to benefit from the lessons life is obviously trying to teach them. But have we earnestly applied ourselves to benefiting from our own? If we are able to accept at least some of the suffering in our lives as largely created by our own behaviour and let it go, chalk it up to experience and move on; if we can begin to see that whatever it was like in the past, we can take control even if we simply choose to accept the inevitable rather than fight it, we reduce our pain quite dramatically. We may even find that our example is what actually inspires those we would so much like to help to do the same, rather than any conviction that we 'know what is best' for them or that we 'are only doing this for their own good.'

It is only with an over-view that the patterns of meaning can be perceived, that what comes into being as a result of suffering and pain can be appreciated. We cannot know in the midst of our sufferings what the end result will prove to be, what is actually being created out of our willingness to endure and be strong. If the pain is caused by others, our confusion and bewilderment is even worse.

The 'Sight' reveals, as the student continues to work with it, that it is not a matter of 'seeing' but accepting an advance philosophy of living. Even in cases of deliberate harm, inflicted cruelty and inhuman behaviour there are no boundaries, no judgements to be made.

For all, at this moment, is as it should be. 'Everything Matters and yet Nothing Matters'.

This book cannot even begin to explain these concepts and the beginner will in any case find them very difficult to comprehend. Further work and study as well as on-going practice will be needed.

We think of cruelty and the inflicting of pain as the most complete expression of evil. But what is evil but our own dark shadow, the complement to our aspirant selves? We all contain the potential for evil as we contain the potential for good and the 'Sight' recognise this and accepts it. Evil, like good, is in the end a choice made and each individual must make that choice himself. What the 'Sight' does is to reveal evil and suffering not as some kind of external enemy to be feared, but as a necessary part of the whole. We could all be evil and the fact that we are not is because we have made a personal choice to try to live in the way we believe to be right. The 'Sight' accepts all moral and ethical codes and teachings, however, and then passes beyond them.

Its greatest revelation is that though nothing can be altered and all is as it should be, yet everything is possible.

142

1	28	121	192	250	308	351	386	417
2	35	123	193	251	310	352	388	418
3	39	124	195	252	311	353	390	419
4	40	132	198	257	312	354	392	421
5	41	136	203	258	317	355	393	422
6	42	148	208	259	318	357	394	423
7	54	149	212	262	320	359	395	425
8	55	154	216	263	321	360	396	427
9	61	157	220	268	322	361	397	428
10	64	160	224	269	324	362	399	429
11	68	164	227	272	326	363	400	431
12	69	166	232	273	327	364	401	432
13	78	167	233	274	328	366	403	433
14	79	168	234	279	331	368	404	435
15	80	169	237	285	333	372	405	436
16	84	172	238	288	336	373	406	437
17	85	174	240	295	337	374	407	438
18	90	175	241	297	338	375	408	440
19	99	180	242	299	341	376	409	441
20	100	182	243	301	344	377	410	442
21	101	183	244	303	347			
23	110	188	247	304	348			
24	119	189	249	307	350			

447	470	493	516	539	562	585	608	631
448	471	494	517	540	563	586	609	632
449	472	495	518	541	564	587	610	633
450	473	496	519	542	565	588	611	634
451	474	497	520	543	566	589	612	635
452	475	498	521	544	567	590	613	636
453	476	499	522	545	568	591	614	637
454	477	500	523	546	569	592	615	638
455	478	501	524	547	570	593	616	639
456	479	502	525	548	571	594	617	640
457	480	503	526	549	572	595	618	641
458	481	504	527	550	573	596	619	642
459	482	505	528	551	574	597	620	643
460	483	506	529	552	575	598	621	644
461	484	507	530	553	576	599,	622	645
462	485	508	531	554	577	600	623	646
463	486	509	532	555	578	601	624	647
464	487	510	533	556	579	602	625	648
465	488	511	534	557	580	603	626	649
466	489	512	535	558	581	604	627	650
467	490	513	536	559	582	605	628	651
468	491	514	537	560	583	606	629	652
469	492	515	538	561	584	607	630	653